ON THE JOB

An Omaha Police Officer's Story: 1958-88

ON THE JOB

An Omaha Police Officer's Story: 1958-88

VERN HAUGER

Omaha Lieutenant Badge #3 (retired)

My-Ver Publishing

Omaha, NE

ISBN: 978-1-936840-28-1
LCCN: 2012942738

My-Ver Publishing
13518 L Street
Omaha, NE 68137

Disclaimer: The stories in this book are true to the best recollection of the author in his experience as an officer during his thirty-year tenure in the Omaha Police Department. Some of the names and situations have been altered to protect privacy.

Front cover: Sergeant Vern Hauger, September 1980. Used with permission from the *Omaha World-Herald*.

Printed in the United States of America.
10 9 8 7 6 5 4 3 2 1

To my wife, Myrta Mae, and our four sons. Myrt made this book happen. For years she urged me to write a book about my experiences as a police officer so our boys would know what I did while I was away from home—on the job. Without her urging, this book would never have been written, and I would not have been able to share these experiences with you.

FOREWORD

In August 1978, twenty-seven recruit officers reported to duty for their first day as Omaha Police Officers. I had the dubious distinction of being the youngest in the class. To say I was probably the most petrified of all is an understatement.

The training staff was intimidating, to say the least. The lieutenant had a glare of sheer intimidation. The other instructors were all seasoned veterans. They had their own ways of making me and the others doubt if we'd make it through training or, if we did, if we could actually survive on the streets.

Then there was Vern Hauger. As the training sergeant, Vern (and it's hard for me not to call him Sergeant Hauger) used a great sense of humor and tact to teach us, mold us, and make our class one of the most successful in recent history.

Vern commanded respect from all, but he didn't have to bully and intimidate us to earn it. It came naturally.

He provided a sense of stability and guidance during our grueling thirteen-week training program.

Shortly after our training started, Vern was scheduled to conduct a class on "death notifications." During my career I've had the unfortunate duty to deliver terrible news to husbands, wives, mothers, and fathers. This is extremely difficult and stressful for any officer.

I'll never forget Vern entering the classroom, standing at the lectern, and saying, "Okay, this is how you do it. You knock on the door. The wife answers the door. You ask her, 'Are you the widow Brown?' She says no. You look her straight in the face and say, 'You are now!' Then you leave."

The class was silent, and then we burst out laughing. This was my first exposure to the use of sick humor in cop culture, which actually is a form of mental therapy we've all used during our careers to keep us from going stark raving mad. Vern then composed himself and gave a very professional course on how to properly tell someone a loved one has just been killed.

Vern's stories of law enforcement in the 1950s through 1980s are truly fascinating. Officers now have access to 800-megahertz radio systems, global positioning satellites, mobile data terminals, and even voice-activated commands for their in-car computers. Vern talks of walking a beat with no radio and receiving his assignments from a call box positioned at either end of his beat. Equipment was antiquated and dilapidated.

Yet Vern's stories show that basic law enforcement then and now are no different. Vern dealt with prostitutes and vagrants in downtown Omaha and saw sexual deviation that only cops can write about. He handled domestic violence calls, homicides, robberies, and investigated horrific car accidents.

How many Omaha Police Officers have actually seen a bad guy fire shots at an occupied Omaha Police cruiser? Vern Hauger has, and this is just one of many harrowing stories he tells so effectively.

Vern Hauger possesses the one quality that is so often lacking among cops. Vern, who grew up dreaming of wearing the uniform, was a cop who prided himself on doing the best job possible in any assignment he worked. Many cops become burned out and fall into the trap of simply making call after call, wanting only to collect a check and go home. Vern was not one of them.

Vern worked many assignments in his career from beat cop, traffic officer, detective, and head of the training unit and crime laboratory. His riveting accounts exemplify the pride and dedication he showed in every call he made, whether it be the young mother cradling her dead baby all the way to the African-American father with two freezing kids in a broken down car who said Vern was the first to stop and help after many simply drove by and looked straight ahead.

Different generations of cops come and go, and although the equipment and training may get better, the basic role of the Omaha Police Officer has never changed. A cop is a cop is a cop, no matter when he or she patrolled the streets of Omaha.

In reading this book I have the impression that Vern's favorite accomplishment was his time leading the training unit. The pages burst with pride in recounting the training of both rookies and seasoned officers. Vern excitedly talks of implementing the Field Training Officer program and designing a more effective shotgun.

There is no way to measure the lives he has impacted, both police and civilian, through his efforts in professionalizing the Omaha Police Department. I can personally attest to this, as I now realize how many things I learned from Vern that became part of my daily routine as an Omaha Police Officer.

Vern and I are a lot alike in that we both dreamed at early ages of becoming Omaha Police Officers, realized that dream, and devoted our lives to being the best officers we could be.

As a kid I was in awe anytime an Omaha Police car cruised down my street. Now I wonder, how many times was the officer in that cruiser Vern Hauger? After reading this book I realize how safe I was when Vern was behind that wheel.

Mark T. Langan
Omaha Police Recruit Class 1-78

[Mark Langan retired from the Omaha Police Department as a sergeant in the narcotics unit. He is now Vice President of Field Operations for the Nebraska Humane Society.]

CONTENTS

INTRODUCTION

Almost as far back as I can remember I wanted to be a police officer. I realize how fortunate I was to have been selected to become one. It never seemed like a job to me. I enjoyed the work, and I was finally doing something that I had always wanted to do.

This book is about some of my personal experiences as I remember them when I was a police officer in Omaha, Nebraska. It covers a thirty-year period from 1958 to 1988.

I started to write this book so my wife and children would know what I did when I was at work. In those days, what police officers did at work stayed at work. We never talked about it except to another officer. My family knew I was a police officer because I put the uniform on every day and strapped the gun belt on my waist before I went out the door, but they never really knew what I did. They might be enlightened when they read this book and find out.

The longer I worked on this book, the more I remembered about the different things I had experienced on the job. Some of the cases I recalled were those that I had tried to suppress, and I thought I had, but now I know it can't be done. One never forgets—no matter how hard we try to.

Technology has changed law enforcement so rapidly since I was a police officer. I know it would be difficult for many of the officers I worked with to function as a police officer today with all of the modern equipment they have. At the same time, many of today's officers would have found it difficult to function in my time without their equipment.

When I came on the job, for example, the radar units used for speed checks were still in their infancy. Breathalyzer tests were not accepted by the courts. Law enforcement agencies were not using the computer yet, and DNA evidence was unheard of.

With today's technology a police officer can now drive through a parking lot at one of the malls and screen every license plate in there while driving by. They will know if any of the cars are wanted or stolen. The technology will also advise the officer who the owners of the vehicles are and if they are wanted for anything.

Law enforcement now has small remote-controlled aircraft (drones) used for surveillance work or traffic enforcement. We have come a long way since I walked my beat with no radio. The only contact I had with the police station was the police call box. There were three of them six blocks apart on my beat. If I didn't report in every hour, they would send a car to check on me.

When I made an arrest, I had to walk the perpetrator to one of the call boxes and call for a cruiser to transport the bad guy to the city jail.

I hope you enjoy a slice of police life back in my day. Those were great years, and I enjoyed every one of them protecting the citizens of Omaha.

- One -

A ROOKIE FULFILLS HIS CHILDHOOD DREAM

As far back as I can remember, growing up in Omaha, I always wanted to be a police officer. I realized that many boys and some girls at one time or another wanted to be either a fireman or a policeman but changed their minds as they grew older. I never changed mine.

I have often thought how fortunate I was to have gotten the job I always wanted. I don't know what I would have done if I had not been able to go into law enforcement. I probably would have done like so many others who worked at jobs they didn't like, and they were miserable most of the time. When I was eighteen in 1953, I enlisted in the Air Force. I wanted to be an air policeman.

The Air Force had a better idea, so I became a stock records specialist sitting at a desk pushing a pencil for the next four years. I did manage to pick up some college credit hours from the University of Maryland while I was in the Air Force.

I had met the love of my life, Myrt, at a July Fourth party, and she still is. We married in 1954 while I was in the Air Force.

When I was separated from active duty in the fall of 1957, I signed up to take the next police exam, which was given a year later in 1958, in the City of Omaha (Nebraska) for the position of police officer with the Omaha Police Department.

Some 640 of us took the written exam. A physical agility test was next, and a background investigation followed. We were given physical and psychological examinations. An oral interview was last. Twenty-four people made it through the testing procedure.

The top twenty men (yes, all men then) were selected to begin their training to become police officers in November. I was among them. We were given a second physical examination, and we still had to complete the training program and a six-month probationary period. We could have been terminated at any time during that period with no right to appeal.

I finished my recruit training and reported to the "A" shift, midnight to 8:00 a.m. in December, working in the cruiser patrol section of the uniform bureau. Our pay was $360 a month. It was called the graveyard shift, and I could understand why.

Roll call was at 11:30 p.m., and we were in our cars by 11:45 p.m. The bars closed at 1:00 a.m. then, and from 2:00 until 5:00 a.m. very little happened and the radio became silent. We checked all of the business buildings to make sure they were still secured.

It was cold that winter, so we had to have the heater turned on in the cruiser, and the noise of the heater fan combined with the heat had a hypnotizing effect on me making me want to sleep. Each night was a struggle to stay awake.

The 1958 police recruit class. Vern Hauger is second from the left in the top row.

I was happy to see spring come, but I still didn't like those hours. But if I wanted the job I had to work them, so I kept my mouth shut and never complained. I have a lot of respect for the people who work that shift. I only had to do it for eight months. Then I was bumped at detail change by someone with more seniority who wanted to work the shift.

I lost fifteen pounds while I was on that shift, and by now, because Myrt and I had a three-year-old son and a new baby at home, I also lost a lot of sleep. I did apprehend my first burglar, however, while on the midnight shift.

We received a radio call of a silent alarm at Louie's Market, a grocery store on the Northwest Radial Highway in the Benson area of the city. An alarm company representative was waiting for us when we arrived at the store. He said the store owner was en route. He told us the interior alarms in the basement kept tripping (turning on) in the different sections of the basement. Since none of the exterior alarms had been tripped, he thought it could be a malfunction in the interior alarm system or a rat in the basement tripping them.

My partner at the time was very knowledgeable when it came to alarms and burglars. He listened to the man and then told him we were going to check the first floor before going into the basement to make sure it was secure and no one was hiding there. He didn't want anyone running out of the building and getting away while we were in the basement.

The first floor checked out fine. My partner had me stay at the top of the stairwell with the shotgun in case someone tried to escape up the stairway while he searched the first half of the basement. When that half was secured, my partner told me to help them search the second half.

I had not gone more than sixty feet when I saw two eyes looking down at me from a shelf that was about three feet above my head. I chambered a round in the shotgun and yelled, "Come down from there."

I was as scared as he was, but I had the shotgun. Once you have heard the sound of a round being chambered in a shotgun, you never forget it. This man had heard it before because he came down in a hurry with both hands up.

I told him to get face down on the floor and to keep his hands above his head where I could see them. My partner yelled, "Did you find someone?"

"Yes," I yelled back. "I have him."

My partner told the alarm representative and the owner to stay where they were while he came over and handcuffed the burglar. We searched the rest of the basement but didn't find anyone else.

An office in the basement had been broken into, and the desk and a file cabinet had been rifled. We checked the shelf where the suspect was hiding and discovered a sack that contained property that had been taken from the office.

The suspect told us he had hidden in the basement of the store when it closed and he had fallen asleep. When he woke up, he broke into the office and looked around. He never realized the basement had alarms in it. When he heard us come into the store, he hid again but we found him.

We never had to go to court on him because he pled guilty to burglary and was sentenced to three years in the state penitentiary.

Even the poorest officer does something better than the other officers do.

I learned a lot on that shift even though I was only on it for a short time. I remember one of our instructors saying even the poorest officer does something better than the other officers do. He said to make note of it and do it the same way. It didn't take me long to see the instructor was right.

- Two -

ON THE BEAT WITH PINK LADIES AND FLOP HOUSES

When I first became a police officer, I was assigned to walk a beat in one of the less desirable parts of our city. I was cast into a world that I had only seen in the movies. Spring was here and the area was once more coming alive. The black people and the white people were returning from the southern states where they had spent the winter. And the Native Americans were returning from their reservations.

Today these people would be called homeless. In those days they were called hobos, tramps, bums, beggars, drunks, and various other names. There were no shelters for them then, so they left to go south for the winter where it was warmer.

Because of vagrancy laws then, most of them spent the winters in jail somewhere working on a chain gang repairing roads and making little rocks out of big ones.

They said it wasn't too bad. They had three hots and a cot (three meals and a place to sleep).

During the summer months while they were in Omaha, some pushed a broom, washed a dish, or panhandled (begged). Most ate out of garbage cans, drank wine, and slept under the stars. They would pool their money in order to have enough to buy a bottle of wine and share it. One never drank more than his share of that bottle. They knew if someone did, it would be the last time anyone shared a drink with the offending party. And everybody knew they needed a drink if they started to get the DT's.

I came across a pink lady party in an alley under a loading dock one night while I was shaking doors to make sure they were locked. A pink lady is a mixture of methyl alcohol and water. They get this alcohol by squeezing it out of the contents of a can of Sterno. Sterno is a brand name for a mixture of gelatinized methyl alcohol and nitrocellulose used as a heat source for small camping stoves and chafing dishes.

This mixture is put in a stocking and the alcohol is rung out of it and mixed with water. It is pink in color and really smells. I believe one can of Sterno will make two quarts of pink lady.

I found four unconscious men under the loading dock that night with one almost empty quart Mason jar and one full of the pink lady mixture. I called the rescue squad for them and somehow they all survived. I offered the squad people a drink but they refused, so I poured it out onto the ground.

One night I found two very drunk Indians under the same loading dock. They were drinking rubbing alcohol cut with water. They had drunk two bottles and were working on the third one when I crashed their party. I told them they were drinking poison. They said they had it before and it didn't kill them. I called the squad for them. I couldn't chance it. I believed they put the skull and crossbones denoting poison on the bottle for a reason. Both of them lived to tell about it, but I still wouldn't try it.

The Indians who lived on my beat must have been getting some type of assistance because they rented the apartments over the stores and they never seemed to work. I know some of the women were turning tricks on the streets. One time some of them received a big payoff from the government for some reason. The money didn't last very long, and they were back to where they had been.

Many of them bought cars that broke down and were towed in by the police. Some of the better cars were repossessed and in three months they were all gone. Some of the Indian families had children who played in the park. Older white people living on Social Security stayed in the apartments over the stores. Some white men lived in the rundown hotels and others rented a cot for the night in one of the two flop houses.

I seldom went into the flop houses if I wasn't called there or if I wasn't looking for someone. They reminded me of an old Army barracks with its row of cots. I think they rented for fifty cents a night, and they had a shower where a renter could clean up. Now that I think about it these people were always clean shaven. Most of them had a safety razor wrapped in a cloth in one of their pockets, so we had to be careful when we reached into any of their pockets when we arrested one of them.

A Chinese family who owned an upscale Chinese restaurant called King Fong's downtown lived in a three-story brick building that stood by itself on one fourth of a block on my beat. Their restaurant was ten blocks from their home, and they walked to work each morning and home again each night. It was a large family of two or more generations, and when they lined up in a row it looked like a parade.

Poppa was first followed by his eldest son down to his youngest son. Momma followed behind the sons and her eldest daughter down to her youngest followed her. They never spoke to each other as they walked. The father might bow to someone now and then, but they never stopped walking. They always went straight to work and home again.

We seldom saw them outside of their home, and they worked most of the time, but they could have had gardens on their roof where they enjoyed themselves. They had to be wealthy people but no one ever bothered them and they never bothered anyone.

This area was truly a melting pot of many different nationalities—Asians, Mexicans, Italians, Native Americans, blacks, and whites. They blended together with few problems. Most of them were considered to be working poor so they had to depend on each other to survive. However being poor didn't stop some of the people from the same race having their disputes. Alcohol was the major cause of most of them.

At first glance you might think most of the businesses in the area were placed there to prey on the weakness of the people living there and to suck the last drop of blood out of them.

My beat was one mile long and two blocks wide. There were two pawn shops, a liquor store, and seven bars. Three of the bars served food. All of the bars were called a working man's bar. They sold mostly whiskey and beer and specialized in boiler makers. The beer on tap was Storz or Falstaff; both were brewed locally.

Every day the liquor store sold a truckload of Old Treasure Muscatel wine, one pint at a time. The bars did siphon off money from the people living there, but they also brought new money to the area, which was spent in other places.

We would load up all the girls who wanted a health "VD" check.

The girls working the streets got some of it. There wasn't much I could do about them except to keep them moving and keep the vice squad informed. They did make some good busts at the hotel but then the girls moved to a new location.

About once a month the police chauffeur would bring the police paddy wagon down to my beat, and we would load up all the girls who wanted a health "VD" check (for venereal disease) into the wagon and take them down to the police station where the city doctor would test them and start their free treatment if any was needed. I can't see them doing anything like that today.

There were a lot of good people who lived in the area. They were prisoners in their homes after the sun went down. They put bars on their doors and windows and pulled their window shades down at night and locked their doors. The street people left them alone because they knew they were armed.

During the day everything was fine. No problems. Most of the residents were older people who owned their homes and could not afford to move. They kept their property up and their old homes looked nice.

When I walked the beat, I developed some good sources for information on what was happening. Years later when I was working as a regional investigator out of the detective bureau, one of these sources gave me some good information on a burglary suspect and the party was arrested and found guilty. A short time later my source was on the job when he fell down an open elevator shaft. I hope it was an accident.

One night I had a call to meet a cruiser with a shooting call in front of a bar that was well known for the activity that took place in there. The victim knew the name of the person who shot him.

The victim said this man who was sitting across from them in the bar might have been with the shooter. They called him Kansas City James. The cruiser officers took the shooting victim to the hospital. I went over to talk to Kansas City James, but he didn't know anything. He wasn't there when the shooting occurred, and he didn't know who the shooter could have been. I knew he was lying to me.

I started to walk away from him, then I turned facing him and said loud enough for everyone to hear, "Thanks

K.C. I thought that's who did the shooting." I got into my car and drove away.

The shooter turned himself in that night. Kansas City James was never seen after that night. He could have gone back to Kansas City or he might have fallen in the river. The shooting victim survived. He wasn't injured as badly as first thought. I recall the shooter did serve some time for this shooting but it wasn't a whole lot.

I didn't have much trouble while I worked there. The people on my beat knew they might need a friend sometime if they had a problem.

One afternoon I saw a cruiser stop at a bar across the street from where I was standing in the shadows under an awning. The officer got out of his car and went in the bar. I walked across the street and went into the bar in time to see the officer give old Andrew a shot to the jaw with his night stick. It was a good hit and it would have knocked a horse down.

Andrew shook his head and raised his fists up like a fighter. I couldn't see the officer's face, but I know he felt fear then and wished he had waited for his backup to arrive like he should have.

"I don't want to hurt you, but I will."

I yelled, "Andrew, are you going to make me hurt you?" When Andrew saw me, I said, "I don't want to hurt you, but I will."

He raised his arms up. He was done.

I told the officer to handcuff him now. His backup came through the door then and I said, "He's all yours," and I left. Old Andy could have whipped both of our butts if he had wanted to, but he knew one did not mess with the beat man.

I met a lot of interesting people when I worked that downtown beat. One was a retired Army master sergeant, but he never told anyone about his military connection. All of his mail went to a post office box. He had a bank account where he saved his money. He would deposit his pension check and draw out enough to pay for a meal ticket, his rent, and a few dollars for himself. He stayed in one of the cheap hotels.

They cleaned his room, changed his towels and sheets, and he didn't have to pay for utilities. His meal ticket was good for thirty meals at one of the greasy spoons where he worked. He was a pearl diver (dishwasher) so he never went hungry.

He said about every four months he would go down to Offutt Air Force Base and catch a hop to some place that he had never been. He stayed in base housing when he could and it didn't cost him much. The old sergeant was living his life the way he wanted, and he was enjoying it to the fullest. He enjoyed his trips and he enjoyed talking to the different people who lived in the hotel.

Another person on my beat had been a medical doctor before the booze took over his life and he lost his license. One man had been an electrical engineer and another one still owned a large sign company that his family ran. They were interesting to talk to when they were sober. Different truck drivers stayed there when they had to lay over waiting for a load, and they were also interesting.

One cold winter night during a snowstorm I found old Amos down and out lying on his back behind the buildings in the alley. The snow was starting to cover him, but his eyes were open and ice crystals were starting to form on them. At first I thought he was dead, but he had a weak pulse and was still warm inside of his coat. I was able to locate a phone and called for a rescue squad to take him to the hospital.

Amos was back on the street in a couple of weeks wiped out of his mind. I put him in jail this time for being drunk in a public place. The judge gave him thirty days in the city jail. He was one of our trusties, so I think he was glad to get out of the cold and have his three hots and a cot.

Fights were common in the bars on the weekends. Every Friday night Shirley and Harvey went to the same bar, and every Friday night they would have a knock-down and drag-out fight. Harvey was the one who got knocked down, yet he never wanted Shirley arrested. I told them I was tired of their fighting, and the next time both of them were going to jail. They both went to jail the next week, but they never fought in that bar again while I was on the beat.

One evening some men were shooting craps in the park. I tried to sneak up on them but someone saw me and they scattered. I never saw anyone move that fast before.

I felt it was time for me to move on after the second winter I had walked the beat in the cold. I needed a change of scenery, so I requested a transfer to a cruiser district at the next detail change. I had been out there on the beat by myself long enough.

I was assigned to a two-man car in a district that included my old beat. It worked out well for me. I knew a lot of the people in the district and that was a plus.

- Three -

A ROOKIE'S FIRST CALLS

March 18, 1959, will always be imprinted on my mind. It was the first time I had ever seen a person with his throat cut. It was shortly after 1:00 a.m., the bars had closed, and the Saint Patrick's Day crowd at the Irish bar on the north side of Farnam Street, east of Fortieth, had spread out into the street. A rumble started, which quickly escalated into one giant brawl.

Several police units were sent in to break it up. When we arrived, most of the fighting had stopped and the crowd was leaving. When we got out of our cruiser, a woman told us that she needed help. My partner asked what was wrong.

She said, "My husband's been cut. He needs to go to the hospital."

Her husband was sitting on the curb looking downward holding his throat. I asked him where he was cut. And when he looked up at me and removed his hands from his throat, I saw what looked to be two mouths—one above his chin and one below it.

He was cut badly, so my partner said, "Let's get him in the car."

I saw what looked to be two mouths—one above his chin and one below it.

The hospital was only six blocks away so we got him there in a hurry. No arteries were cut, but his thyroid gland was severed. Neither he nor his wife saw who cut him because they were busy trying to get out of the crowd.

When I was bumped from the "A" shift (midnight to 8:00 a.m.) to the "C" shift (4:00 p.m. to midnight), I was assigned to the traffic section. Everyone wondered how a rookie like me could get this choice assignment. It was easy since there was an opening in the traffic section and no one put in for it. I was put there because I was bottom man on the seniority list and had no say in the matter.

It was a choice job. I learned a lot about traffic law enforcement and testifying in court during the six months I was there. I enjoyed the work and the people I worked with. When the next detail change came, I was bumped back to the patrol section.

I will never forget the personal injury accident I assisted with while I was on the traffic crew. It was a hot August evening in 1959. The collision involved two cars with minor damage to them, but the driver of one of the cars—a young woman—was thrown out of her car when her driver's door popped open.

One of the cars ran over her abdominal area squishing about two feet of her digestive organs out of her body through her rectum.

She was in a lot of pain, and she said, "I hurt so bad, I think I'm going to die."

I told her she wasn't going to die and tried to calm her down. I held her hand with both of mine and talked to her until the rescue squad got there. I was sure glad to see them. They put wet towels on her intestines and transported her to the hospital. I really didn't think she was going to make it.

I checked on her a few days later when I was at the hospital. They said her worst injury was a fractured pelvis, but she should be okay and had been transferred to a different hospital.

When the next detail change came I was bumped back to the patrol section. I had enough seniority now to stay on the "C" shift; however, I was the utility man for a long time. I didn't mind because it gave me a chance to learn more about the job much faster than my classmates. I worked wherever they needed someone.

I held her hand with both of mine and talked to her until the rescue squad got there.

For example, I was assigned to guard prisoners who were in the hospital until they were well enough to be booked, post bond, or stay in jail. I worked security and crowd control at different functions. I directed traffic downtown during rush hour, and I walked beats.

I got to know a lot of people and some got to know me. Every night was different and exciting, so I looked forward to going to work. I worked every cruiser district in the city filling in for officers on their days off.

When I was finally assigned to my own district in 1961, I was prepared to do the job. My district was Dodge Street north to Cuming Street and Twenty-fourth Street east including East Omaha. East Omaha is located south of the Eppley Airfield and east of Abbott Drive to the Missouri River.

My beat consisted of mostly dirt streets, rundown shanties, two bars, a grocery store, and a lot of outlaws. The airport has since bought most of them out and extended their property to the south along the river. The state built a minimum security prison there, and the Open Door Mission built a new facility. Since most of the people were forced to move, East Omaha is no longer the problem area it once was.

My beat consisted of mostly dirt streets, rundown shanties, two bars, a grocery store, and a lot of outlaws.

I will always remember the first call I received in my own district. It was to assist a woman who had fallen down and couldn't get up. The address turned out to be a second-story flat over a rundown thrift store on North Sixteenth. When I arrived on the call, the woman who phoned the police was waiting at the top of the stairs. She said her neighbor Sadie had slipped and fallen in her bathroom. She tried to help her up but she wasn't strong enough. She showed me into the first apartment on my right and led me to the bathroom.

It was located at the end of a narrow hallway with an equally narrow thirty-inch doorway. I had a hard time believing what I was seeing. Sadie was a big white woman—weighing over 300 pounds. In order for her to use the bathroom, which was too small for her to turn around in, she would back down the hallway, shuffling in her terrycloth house slippers, into the bathroom where she would hike up her dress and drop her panties before sitting down on the toilet stool.

She must have been in a hurry this time because she didn't see her husband, John, sitting on the stool reading his newspaper.

She fell backward mashing him into the toilet stool.

John was a little guy who couldn't weigh 130 pounds. John told me he was interested in a story he was reading and didn't see or hear her until it was too late. As he saw her backing down the hallway, he let out a yell, which scared her causing her to lose her balance. She fell backward mashing him into the toilet stool. He said he could not feel his legs.

The woman and I together were not strong enough to pull Sadie off poor John on the john. I used their phone to call the police radio operator and advised him that I had an injured man and needed the rescue squad.

The squad arrived shortly, and the four of us were able to get Sadie off John and out of the bathroom. She was okay and only her pride was hurt. They carried John out to the living room and checked him over as the feeling was starting to come back into his legs. He too was going to be okay. He could stand up now, so they helped him to his bedroom and we left.

Once we were outside, I thanked the rescue squad for their help. I would be remiss if I didn't tell you I thought I heard someone snicker. I often saw John out walking after that. He would wave and I would wave back. I never saw Sadie again, but I don't think she was able to get down the stairs.

I remember one call to a local hotel where a man had suddenly become very ill, but he was so large that the hotel personnel were not able to get him out of his room. He weighed well over 600 pounds. His room was on the third floor, and it had two large windows that faced the street. The rescue squad people said they could get him out through the window if they could take the window out. The hotel owner told them to take the window out. I don't think he wanted the body left in his room if the man died.

They took the window out and used a small crane mounted on a truck to lift the man out of the room through the window.

They took the window out and used a small crane mounted on a truck to lift the man out of the room through the window and lowered him to the ground where he was put into the ambulance and transported to the hospital. Someone notified the news media of what was going on, and they covered the story. The fire department did a good job, and it was quite impressive. The man never came back to the hotel.

One hot August night my partner and I knew it was going to be a busy shift, so we took our lunch break early because we knew we might not be able to get one later on.

Don't get me wrong, we would not have gone hungry since we could always grab a bite on the run, but we needed the lunch break to catch our breath.

Our assigned cruiser was late in coming in at shift change because they had received a late call. We gave the cruiser a quick inspection for damage and checked our equipment before going into service.

Radio was holding a shoplifter call for us. The suspect had fought with the employees at the store. When we arrived at the store, they told us to hurry because they were holding the suspect in the office at the back of the store. He looked as if he had lost the fight already. We knew the suspect since we had arrested him before.

We handcuffed him and my partner took the report. The man had walked into the store and gone into the back room where he took a case of cigarettes (not a carton but a case) and walked back through the store into the parking lot where he was apprehended.

When we took him downtown for booking, he bragged that he had been doing this once a week for several months and gotten away with it. I don't think you could believe one word the man said.

We had one call after another for the remainder of the night. Our last call was a shooting, which I will always remember. We were only three blocks from where the shooting occurred, but the rescue squad had to come from two miles away. The address led us to one of the large old two-story houses in the area that had been converted into apartments.

A woman with a cordless phone met us at the door. Just inside the entry door in the hallway a man was lying on his back in a pool of blood. His eyes were closed and he was moaning "oh" over and over. A sawed-off 12-gauge shotgun was lying on the floor by him.

The woman dialed someone and she said, "Hello, Erma, I just shot Willie."

We handcuffed her and had her sit in a chair. My partner advised her of her rights. She said Willie had been "fooling around with some bitch," and she was going to get her too.

The rescue squad rushed in. One of the first things they did was to cut Willie's trousers off him. He had a hole in his lower abdominal area about the same size as a 12-gauge shotgun barrel. The hot blast seared the entrance wound so there was little blood there. They rolled him over and found a larger hole in his back with about two feet of his shredded intestine hanging out of it, and there was a lot of blood.

They took him to the hospital. And we took her and the shotgun to the detective bureau. We finished up our reports on the way to the police station.

About a week later I was at the hospital and asked about Willie. He had gone home. He lost his appendix, some of his intestines, and a unit of blood, but doctors were able to sew him back together again, and he was almost as good as new.

The police department required us street officers to report for duty thirty minutes before our roll call time so we could copy the daily bulletin and stolen auto sheet. I tried to get there earlier so I would have time to talk with the guys and get the latest scoop. Seven of my classmates from the academy were working this shift, and we swapped a lot of war stories.

Use caution as this guy was considered dangerous.

One spring day in 1961 there was an item in the daily bulletin about a party wanted for murder in Boston. I thought it was rather odd that we would have it on our bulletin, but I copied the information down. The bulletin said to use caution as this guy was considered dangerous. He had a tattoo on his right forearm of a bleeding heart with a dagger stuck through it with the letters WML below it.

My partner, Don, had to direct traffic downtown that night, so I advised radio that I was dropping him off and I would be working a one-man car until further notice.

Radio gave me a call to see a party in one of the downtown jewelry stores about a suspicious customer. The owner met me at the door and said a man in his store "was up to no good." He had watched him go into the pawn shop two doors away. I went into the pawn shop and only one person was in there. His back was to me and he was talking to the owner of the pawn shop who was in the caged area where the high-dollar items are located.

As this patron reached up with his right hand and took hold of the cage, I saw a bleeding heart tattoo with a dagger stuck in it and the letters WML on his forearm.

"Don, keep him covered while I put the cuffs on him."

Astonished, I drew my service revolver and shoved it hard into the man's back as I yelled, "Police. Don't move. We have you covered." I don't know why but I then said, "Don, keep him covered while I put the cuffs on him."

I got him down on his knees and gave him a pat down. He was clean. The pawn shop owner stood back, his eyes were as big as saucers. I told him to call the police station and get me some back up. This was before we had the portable radios or cell phones. It didn't take long for help to arrive.

This was the wanted party. When he saw that I was alone, he said, "If I knew you were alone, you'd a never taken me."

Two detectives arrived and said they would transport the suspect to the station and for me to bring my reports to them. I never heard any more about the case until years later when I learned the two detectives had an all-expenses-paid trip to Boston to testify at the guy's trial. They must have taken credit for my arrest. It would not have been the first time something like this happened.

One slow night, about ten, radio called the car number I was driving, so I answered the call with our car number and our location. Radio gave us a call to obtain a report of a missing child and the address. I told them we were clear on the call, and radio answered with our car number and the time, 2150 hours.

When we arrived at the house, all of the outside lights were turned on. A younger woman answered the door and she was frantic. She said she put her seven-year-old son in bed at nine and at nine thirty when she checked on him he was gone. While my partner took the report, I checked the house for the child. I looked in all of the closets, under his bed, and in the basement. I checked in their car that was in the attached garage.

I noticed a large dog house in the back yard. Because I had looked everywhere else, I shined my flashlight into it.

A big yellow lab raised her head and looked at me. The boy was in the dog house with her—sound asleep. I turned off my light and went back into the house. I told the woman I found something in the back yard that I wanted her to look at. My partner had just finished the report so he came along.

It was times like this that made the job so rewarding.

I turned on my flashlight and shined it in the dog house. She saw her son then and fell to her knees and reached into the dog house and picked him up. The dog looked at her as if to say what are you doing? The woman was crying as she thanked me. It was times like this that made the job so rewarding.

My partner tore up the report since it was no longer needed. We hit back in service, and radio gave us a call about a drunk disturbance. When we arrived on the call, a very intoxicated man was telling this woman that he was going to drive their car home. At that time we could arrest someone for being drunk in a public place.

I escorted the party to the back seat of the cruiser on the passenger's side, but he refused to put his right leg in the cruiser. My partner closed the door firmly on his leg and told him to get it in the car. The man told my partner where he could go and bated us by saying, "Try it again." The woman said, "He has an artificial leg." The man laughed and put his leg in the car.

We had another drunk on our beat who had two artificial legs, and you had to watch him. If you took your eyes off him for one second, he would deck you. He was a mean person. Most of the policemen that knew this had learned it the hard way.

When I left a unit it would be in better shape than it had been when I first arrived there.

Most of the officers on this shift were exceptional, and they taught us rookies a lot about police work. Out of our class of twenty recruits there were twelve of us who eventually retired from the job. Our class did well: one was a captain, two were lieutenants, and nine were sergeants.

I had two goals I wanted to reach while I was on the job before I retired. One was to be a police lieutenant on the day shift, and the other one was when I left a unit it would be in better shape than it had been when I first arrived there.

I managed to reach both of my goals and I learned a little from everyone I worked with. I always tried to practice the Golden Rule: "Do unto others as you would have others do unto you." Some of the people I had to deal with mistakenly thought this was a weakness on my part, and I would have to switch to plan "B," which was to be firm and "do unto others before they do unto you." It worked out well for me as I fulfilled my childhood dream to become a police officer.

- Four -

IT WAS A REAL CIRCUS

At 11:15 p.m. one night I was sitting by the police call box finishing my daily report. It was 1962. They would be calling me in for shift change at 11:30 p.m. We had to use the call box to show we were still in our district when we were called in.

Suddenly the radio went crazy. The circus was in town and someone had turned all of the lions loose when the patrons were leaving the circus. I listened as car after car was dispatched to check the report of a lion being seen somewhere in the downtown area. Lions loose in the city! What would be next?

I had escorted elephants, rounded up crazed range cattle, and herded hogs, but I never had to deal with an African lion.

When radio called my car number, I answered a call to check the report of a lion in a stairwell in an alley. When I arrived on the call, people were standing there blocking the alley entrance.

Someone asked, "Is there a lion down there?"

I said, "I'm going to find out when I go down there. If there is one, it's liable to run this way, so if I were you people, I wouldn't be blocking the alley."

The lion looked scared, and I know I was too.

They moved back and I entered the alley in my cruiser. I stopped at each stairwell and got out of the car and checked it with my flashlight. Midway through the block, I found the lion. She was lying in the dark at the bottom of the stairwell. The lion looked scared, and I know I was too. I had never been this close to a lion before without bars or glass between us.

I blocked the stairwell with the cruiser and advised radio. Soon after that a truck pulling a circus trailer came down the alley. The passenger got out, looked in the stairwell, and said something in German. I backed the cruiser up so they could push the trailer up to the stairwell and raise the tailgate.

The trainer said something else in German, and the lion came up the staircase on the run and jumped into the trailer. The man dropped the tailgate, and they had her so they left to get another one.

I was happy and hit 10-7 (out of service) to the garage where I finished my daily report. We were very lucky all of the lions were captured and no one was hurt.

We had a bad winter that year—just one snowstorm after another—and the snow removal crews were not able to keep up with it. Their snow removal equipment was breaking down faster than they could repair it. The city decided to prioritize which streets would be plowed first down to which ones would be plowed last. The secondary streets in the hilly parts of the city were plowed last since this area was the hardest on their equipment.

The Nebraska Guard loaned some four-wheel-drive ambulances to the city for the fire department to use in these areas. I won't tell you which area I lived in, but I had to wade through some deep snow for six blocks before I reached a plowed street where a cruiser could pick me up so I could get to work.

Like postal workers, we braved the cold and the heat. When the cruiser district I wanted opened up, I bid on it. I got the district and a new cruiser came with it. The car had air conditioning. This was the first year our cars were air conditioned, and this happened to be one of the first cars put in service. It didn't have a hundred miles on the odometer when I left the garage with the windows rolled up and a big smile on my face.

I hadn't gone ten miles when I was driving down a winding road and something happened. I turned the steering wheel to navigate a curve, but the car went straight ahead. I slammed on the brakes and stopped before I ran off the roadway. I could spin the steering wheel in either direction, but the front wheels didn't respond.

I hit out of service and called for the police tow truck. They wanted to know the nature of the tow, and I said the steering went out. You could hear the officers clicking their radio mics. This was their way of saying ha, ha because my new car broke down, and they were also telling me welcome to the crew. If they didn't like me, no one would have clicked their radio mics.

The tow truck driver discovered the pitman arm in the steering system was defective and had broken. My new car was towed in, and I had to drive a replacement vehicle that was worn out. The front seat was broken down so much, I had to sit on a board that covered the hole in the driver's seat. The engine didn't run well. And, of course, there was no air conditioning.

The next night I had my new car back, the AC was working, and I was happy again.

There were three older women in my district who had no families and lived alone. Their neighbors looked after them the best they could, but they would soon be in need of more care than the neighbors could give them.

One woman told me someone was getting into her house and taking the screws out of her sewing machine and replacing them with rusty ones. I asked her if she had a screwdriver. She got me one and I tightened all of the visible screws so no one could get them out. Then we made sure all of her doors and windows were locked.

I told her not to let anyone in her house that she didn't know. I told her to check her doors and windows every day to make sure they were locked. I said I would drive by and watch her house. I never had a call from her again. Later I saw in the paper that she had passed away.

The second woman reported that a black helicopter was bothering her. They would fly low over her house and hover outside her windows looking into her house. Other times they would shine bright lights in her windows. They never tried to get in, but she just knew they were spying on her. She knew the Kennedys had sent them.

I asked her if she had any aluminum foil. I told her to tape a piece of foil on each of her windows. It didn't have to be very big. A five-inch by five-inch piece would work fine. The next time they tried to shine a light in her window, the foil would reflect back into their eyes and blind them. I told her they would go away and never bother her again.

I told her to tape a piece of foil on each of her windows.

I noticed she had put the foil on her windows. It must have worked because I never got another call from her.

The third woman was a sweet little lady who said the neighborhood boys were climbing in the trees in her front yard. She said, when she asked them to stop, they turned into little monkeys and they laughed at her. I told her, "You can't talk to monkeys because they will just laugh at you."

She had a garden hose on a reel sitting there with a nozzle on it all hooked up to the sill cock. I reached down and pulled her garden hose off the reel and told her to spray them with the hose. I said it won't hurt them, but they don't like it and they will really scatter. I said, "They might not ever come back. If they do come back, spray them again and they will leave."

She never called back either.

A couple of years later my wife and I were driving past her house and saw her in the front yard spraying water high up in the trees.

Even today when I drive past her house I have visions of her spraying the monkeys out of her trees.

I was twenty-two years old when I was separated from military service. I had been halfway around the world and thought I had seen it all. After being on the police department less than six months, I realized that I hadn't seen anything. I soon learned that the human animal can be the most unpredictable creature on this planet.

It was two in the morning in June 1959 when a woman in a white wedding dress first appeared in our headlight beams. Blood covered the front of her gown and she was crying.

Her face was swollen and she appeared to have been beaten up. She said her new husband did it to her. After their wedding reception at one of our local hotels, they went up to their room. Her husband had too much to drink and they got into an argument, which quickly turned into a fight. He punched her several times before she could get away. She had run out of the room and left her purse, money, and clothing there.

She didn't want him arrested. She just wanted to get her property and leave. We took her to the hotel and got a room key and escorted her to her room. The groom was sleeping on the bed in his clothes, and he never woke up.

We gathered up her stuff and left. Her car was in the parking lot so we helped her load it. She thanked us for helping her and watched as she got in her car and drove away. My partner who was single at the time looked at me and said, "I wonder how long that marriage will last?"

One morning around five, we took our lunch break at the train station. It was in the early 1960s, and the passenger trains were still operating, but there weren't many passengers anymore. When we were getting back in our car, an older couple climbed into the back seat, and the man said, "Please take us to [a certain address]."

My partner and I looked at each other, and my partner said, "This taxi only goes to the city jail."

"This taxi only goes to the city jail."

The man's face turned red as he realized they were not in a cab. He said, "I'm sorry, I thought this was a taxicab."

We laughed and my partner told them to stay in the car because we were going that way. I'll bet that was one cab ride they remembered for a long time.

Shortly after, I received a radio call to see a lady about a snake in her apartment.

I don't like snakes, but I had to answer the call. I asked her how the snake got into her apartment on the second floor of the building. She said her son brought it home. The boy looked to be about ten years old, and he had a big grin on his face. The snake in the kitchen was a little garter snake about two feet long. I told her it was not poisonous but that she might need a tetanus shot if one bit her.

"Take the snake outside and don't bring any more of them in the apartment," I told the boy. I had saved face and the snake was gone.

Two weeks before I was due to get my discharge from the Air Force Reserves in August 1962, I received a notice to stand by for recall to active duty. This could not be happening to me. I would have to go if I was recalled. There was no way I could get out of going,

We had just built a new house. Myrt and I talked it over and decided I would stay in the Air Force if I were recalled because I could retire in a few years. Two weeks later I received a large envelope from the Air Force Reserves that contained my discharge papers. Someone at the reserve center had a weird sense of humor in sending me the recall notice. I laugh today, but I wasn't laughing then.

- Five -

ALL IN A NIGHT'S WORK— EVEN A NAKED GUY

I enjoyed working the "C" shift, 4:00 p.m. to midnight, because the time went by so fast it was time to go home before I realized it. The work load could be heavy, but it was never boring. Many robberies occurred on the "C" shift.

One summer, the same guy held up several ice cream stores. We had a store in our district that sat in a secluded area. My partner and I both thought it would be robbed, so we gave it special attention for most of the summer, but for some reason a robbery never happened.

One especially hot night we headed for the ice cream store. We were going to cool off with a milkshake. When I turned into their driveway, a man ran out of the store at full speed and collided head-on with a man who was walking up to the door. They both went down, and the man who had run out of the store wasn't getting up.

The manager of the store came out then and yelled, "That man just robbed me."

"That man just robbed me."

We handcuffed the suspect while he was still dazed and patted him down. He wasn't armed, but he had the store's money in one of their sacks on him. The man he ran into said he wasn't hurt. I hit out of service on the radio at our location with a robbery call. We took the suspect back into the store where we completed our reports before taking him to the detective bureau at central police headquarters.

Everyone on our crew thought we did some good police work. We didn't tell them any differently. We said we just happened to be in the right place at the right time. We didn't say anything about the milkshakes we almost had.

Less than six months later I was working in a different district with a different partner when we received a hold-up-in-progress-call at the grocery store at Sixteenth and Locust streets. We were right on top of this one. As we approached the store from the south, we saw the stick-up man run out of the store. He had his gun in one hand and a sack of money in the other. He saw us and turned to the north running away from us.

He ran in front of the store and down an alley. We jumped out of the cruiser with our guns drawn. We yelled for him to stop. As we drew down on him, he seemed to explode. His arms shot straight out and his gun went flying one direction and the money sack went the other way. The air was full of money floating in the air.

An employee of the store who knew nothing of the robbery was dumping trash in the dumpster behind the store when he heard us yell. He said he looked around the corner of the building and he saw us with our guns drawn. This robber was running straight at him, so he clobbered him with his heavy-duty 32-gallon commercial-grade trash can.

It worked out well for everyone, and he might have even saved the robber's life. I know he saved my partner and me from having to make a lot of reports, and he received an award from his employer.

We cuffed the suspect and took him back into the store where he was identified. We made our reports and transported the suspect to the detective bureau at central police headquarters. The suspect had been released from the Colorado State Prison just three days prior to the hold-up. We were very lucky the way things worked out that night.

When we hit back in service, our next call was to see a lady about a barking dog. I jokingly asked my partner if he thought he could handle it. We never knew what the next call might be, but that is what made the job so interesting. Every day was different and exciting.

While patrolling in the warehouse district, I once observed an automatic washing machine carton with two bare legs sticking out of the bottom of it walking very cautiously toward me on the railroad tracks. Every now and then he would stop and raise the box to see where he was going. The man in the box was stark naked.

Just when I thought I had seen everything, something like this happened. The man told me he had been robbed by two men at knife point. They took everything he had including his clothing. I remembered seeing an old Army blanket in the trunk of the cruiser. I got it for him and took a report of the robbery.

> The man in the box was stark naked.

He may have been telling me the truth or he could have left his clothing in someone's bedroom when he had to make a quick exit. I will never know. I took him to the Salvation Army where they gave him some clothing.

I believe it was in the summer of 1962 I had a new recruit officer with me who had been in the Marine Corps just prior to coming on the police force. He was a sharp young man whom I felt was going to be a good officer. It was around 9:00 p.m. when radio put out a call of shots being fired about four miles south and two miles west of us. Then a second call came out about a party in a blue car who had just shot a girl on her front porch. He was headed our direction.

I told the recruit to start going west. Radio hit the beeper; three more teenage girls were shot standing on a street corner. He was still coming our way, so I told my young partner to step on it. Another radio call pinpointed another party shot a dog three blocks south of us and one block to the west.

I told my partner to slow down, which he did, and the blue car flew through the intersection crossing right in front of us going north at about 60 mph. I turned on the red lights and siren and said, "Let's get him."

I advised radio that we were in pursuit of the shooter and gave our direction and location. I advised my partner to slow down because the road makes a square turn to the left just ahead, and the guy wouldn't be able to make it as fast as he was going.

Sure enough, the car was on its top and the gun was sticking out from underneath the car. The shooter was out of the car frantically trying to pull the gun loose from under the car. I grabbed our shotgun out of its rack and ran toward him. He turned facing me still trying to get the gun loose.

Car was on its top and the gun was sticking out from underneath the car.

I gave him a quick upper cut to his chin with the butt end of my shotgun, and it was all over. He was out like a light. I cuffed him and told my partner to call for a rescue squad. I told him I wanted him to ride in the squad with the suspect, and that the handcuffs don't come off for any reason.

I said I would be out to the hospital as soon as I finished up at the scene, but it would be quite a while. I called for the crime lab to take pictures and a tow truck to take the car to our lot. I finished my reports and went to the hospital to pick up my partner.

He told me the little girl who had been shot had died, and they were going to hold the shooter at the hospital for observation. An officer was being sent out to guard him. When relief arrived, I retrieved my handcuffs. He had used his to cuff the suspect to the bed. We went to the station and turned in our reports to the detective bureau captain. He checked them over and signed them. We were done for the night.

My recruit had quite a story to share with his classmates the next day.

- Six -

SUICIDE CALLS

Things were back to normal for a few days after the car chase when we nabbed the shooter, and then I got a call to see a party about her ex-boyfriend who was sitting in his car in front of her apartment.

My partner was directing rush hour traffic downtown at the time. I went alone and met the woman on the corner about two blocks away from her apartment. She said she had been coming home from work on a city bus when she was getting off at her stop and noticed her ex-boyfriend sitting in his car parked in front of her apartment building. So she told the driver she couldn't get off because he was there. The bus driver called his dispatcher who in turn called the police. (No one had cell phones at that time.)

She was afraid of her ex-boyfriend. She said he had changed so much since they broke up she didn't know what he might do next. I had her get in the cruiser and drove around the two blocks to park behind him. I told her to wait in the car while I talked to him.

I saw the hose coming out of the exhaust pipe going up to the window on the right rear door.

I noticed his head was lying back on the seat. Then I saw the hose coming out of the exhaust pipe going up to the window on the right rear door. The car's engine was running. I ran back to the cruiser and called radio. I asked for a rescue squad at my location and told them I had a party who was overcome by carbon monoxide.

I ran back to the car and found the driver's door unlocked. I opened the door, reached in for the key, and turned off the ignition. The exhaust smell was strong, and the guy was not breathing. His face was blue and his lips almost black. His arms and hands were also black up to his elbows.

I held my breath as I reached into the car and dragged him out. I lost my grip, and he fell onto the pavement. This was before they taught mouth-to-mouth resuscitation. I was able to roll him over on his stomach and position his arms and turn his head. I straddled him as I was taught and pressed down on his back. There was no resistance; the air came out. I pulled up on his elbows, which was the rescue technique we were taught then. I didn't know if any air went in. I pressed down on his back again, and the air came out, so it must have worked.

I repeated this procedure over and over. I was about to stop when he suddenly gasped for air and started breathing on his own, at which time he became deathly sick and started vomiting. The rescue squad people had arrived and took care of him while I told them what I had done.

They took him to the hospital. I towed his car in for safekeeping and was finishing my reports when a detective showed up. He was assigned to do the follow-up on this call. I gave him my reports, and he said he would take them in for me. It was time to pick up my partner. I felt good about what I did.

Four days later I read in the paper where this same guy was successful in committing suicide. He shot himself in the head. His ex-girlfriend didn't have to worry about him now. He wouldn't be bothering her any more.

I was surprised by the number of suicide calls I received on the job over the years. Most were older people, but each year it seemed as if more young people were doing it.

Most women will not commit suicide by shooting themselves in the head; however, they would shoot themselves in the heart or chest. Women will seldom hang themselves either. Some dress up in their very best clothes, fix their hair, and put makeup on before they swallow a bunch of pills or tape a plastic bag over their heads. Women leave longer notes than men, and they seem to commit suicide on a birthday or holiday. It is my belief they do this so families will remember the day they ended their lives.

Men not only shoot themselves in the head, as the ex-boyfriend finally did, but they often go to great lengths to do it. Most shotguns are too long for a guy to put the barrel against his head or in his mouth and reach the trigger. They will take their shoe off and use their big toe to push the trigger or get a stick long enough for them to reach the trigger and push it with their hand. Unlike a woman, men will hang themselves or jump off a building.

I was less than a block away from the house when I got the call about a possible suicide. A rescue squad was on the way. When I entered the house, several children were screaming and crying, "My mother killed herself."

Mom was in the kitchen lying on the floor on her back. Her head rested in a pool of blood. She had shot herself above the right temple, and the bullet came out on the left side of her head. I picked up the revolver she used—a Colt .38-caliber police special. The rescue squad people were there checking her over.

Blood was flying in all directions.

I went in the next room to get the information I needed for my report from her ten-year-old son.

Suddenly the woman was up fighting with the rescue squad people. Blood was flying in all directions. Both hers and theirs. They were finally able to restrain her and take her to the hospital. The kids were happy mommy wasn't dead. A neighbor was going to stay with the children. She had called their father, and he was going to stop at the hospital and then come home.

I talked to the doctor at the hospital. He said the bullet had struck her head at just the right angle to cause it to follow her skull over the top of her head and come out on the other side. All it did was knock her out. He said they were going to keep her in the hospital for a couple of days. I phoned the detective bureau and brought the reports in to them.

Another time, my partner and I had made several disturbance calls to the same address. The family who lived there consisted of three people: the father and mother and one child. The father was in his late sixties, the mother in her late thirties, and the child was a boy about fifteen. The father, who appeared to be of average intelligence, was a brakeman for the railroad. The mother was severely retarded, and the son who had some problems was an electronics wizard. He put a sound system in their house that was second to none. He built some of the component parts himself.

The first time we had contact with the family, the boy had beaten his mother, and when the father came home from work and saw what the boy had done, he tore into him. The boy stood six feet two and weighed in at 300 pounds. Dad bit off more than he bargained for, and the boy gave him several good licks before he retreated to the basement.

We took the boy to the youth center. There was no talking to him that night because he was so strung out. They kept him at the youth center for a month and sent him home with some medication.

About a month later he decided he didn't need his medication and destroyed the house. When we arrived there, he calmed down some but there was no talking to him. He didn't want any part of our big brother crap. We told him he had to go to the youth center again. We said he could go the easy way or the hard way; it didn't matter to us.

We said, "If you choose the hard way, you're going to get hurt and you're going to be in the hospital for a long time. We are not your parents so don't do anything stupid."

He put his hands behind his back and we cuffed him.

"If you choose the hard way, you're going to get hurt."

Around five weeks later we received another call to their house to make an investigation. We wondered which one of his parents was dead. But they were both waiting outside by the front door.

"It's our son," they said, "he's in the basement."

Their sound system was blaring; music was playing throughout the house. We went downstairs and couldn't believe what we were seeing.

The boy had hung himself by the neck from one of the steel water pipes in the ceiling. He was nude except for a loin cloth he had fashioned out of one of the drapes. He had shaved off all of his hair and painted his whole body a light green color. The rope around his neck was short enough that his toes were just above the floor after he had stepped off a chair.

We cut him down and called the detective bureau. What a pity this had to happen. This one bothered me.

Sometimes, the suicides weren't as clear-cut. I received a call to meet a cruiser on a call about a suicide. When I arrived, the officers said the deceased was found hanging from the banister on the staircase going from the first floor to the second floor. He had taken his shoes off and stood on one of the dining room chairs. He had taken his belt off and looped it around two of the balusters on the banister about seven feet above the floor.

He had put the belt under his chin and pulled it up tight around his neck. He had inserted the prong through the hole in the belt to hold it tight and placed the loose end of the belt through a belt loop on the belt. Then he stepped off the chair. The belt was made out of thick leather and it was one and a half inches wide with a heavy steel buckle on it.

The man's wife and daughter found him hanging there when they came home from grocery shopping. He had left a note saying he was sorry, but he was tired of life and it was time for him to move on.

When the officers removed the belt from his neck, they noticed a bruise about the width of a clothesline rope going around his neck. They didn't like the looks of it, so they called for an investigator. Could someone have strangled him and then tried to cover it up by making his hanging look like a suicide? These two women could not have done it. They were not physically able to lift the man that high.

I asked them if he had ever tried to do this before. They said yes about a week before but they were home then and they had cut him down. He had used a clothesline rope then.

When I asked for more details, they said he had been despondent and was seeing a doctor for it. I asked if he had gone to the hospital then. They said yes they called the police who took him to the hospital. Doctors kept him there for three days and changed his medication. They thought he was doing better. They said they never would have gone to the store if they hadn't thought it would be all right.

I told the officers I was going out to my car to check out what the daughter had told me. Every detail was confirmed. I told the officers they had done a good job in noticing the bruise marks and following up on it.

I investigated one suicide in 1975 on Thanksgiving Day, which was a typical textbook case. The person who committed suicide was a white female in her late seventies. She left a long note saying why she ended her life and blamed her daughter. She wanted her daughter and her family over for Thanksgiving dinner at noon, but they were going to the son-in-law's parents' home for dinner. They had asked the mother to come with them, but the mother refused and asked them to come over to her place around six and they could have coffee with her.

She looked dead and they saw the carving knife in the tub and the blood.

When they got to the mother's home, no one answered the door so the daughter used her key and went inside. They heard water running in the bathroom. The daughter knocked on the door and yelled, "Mom, are you in there?"

No one answered so she opened the door. Her mother was in the bathtub slumped face forward over the faucets and the water was running. She pulled her up and called for her husband. Together they sat her up. She looked dead and they saw the carving knife in the tub and the blood. Her wrists were cut. They called the rescue squad.

The 911 operator sent a cruiser with the rescue squad and they called me. The woman was still in the tub. Her hair had recently been done and she was wearing fresh makeup. She was wearing a business suit and hose. I checked her wrists and both had hesitation marks on them.

Before a person cuts her wrist, she will often make a test cut called a "hesitation mark." Then they will either stop or go ahead and cut their wrists. People who attempt to commit suicide by cutting their wrists usually fail for different reasons. This lady didn't fail. She almost severed her left hand and she had run cold water over her wrists to deaden the pain, and it also helped the blood flow by not letting it clot.

I asked the daughter if her mother always dressed this way around home. She said no she only dressed this way to go to church. I called the crime lab for pictures, and then I called the coroner. He said there was no need for an autopsy and wanted to know what funeral home they used and he would call them. The crime lab took their pictures, the body was removed, and I finished my report.

I talked to the daughter and her husband for a while before I left. This was a typical example of one way a female commits suicide. It was as if she had a checklist and went down it checking everything off. She made my job a lot easier with her note and the way she dressed up, but I felt sorry for her daughter.

The easiest suicide I ever investigated was in the fall of 1975. A security guard shot himself in the head while he was in bed using his service revolver, a .38-caliber police special. He left a handwritten note that said, "Take my remains to the John A Gentleman Mortuary" and signed it.

The crime lab did all of the work on this case. They found traces of gunshot residue on the man's hand. They recovered a bullet from the mattress, which came from his revolver, and handwriting analysis proved the note was written by the deceased. Suicide. Case closed.

- Seven -

LESSON: USE THE NIGHT STICK, NOT THE SAP

When I put my name in for day shift at detail change, this time I was sure I would get it because I knew I had more time on the job than some of the people who were working the day shift. It had been over five years since I worked a day job. I couldn't believe the number of older officers who were still patrolling the streets on the day shift.

Since there was no mandatory retirement age at that time, many officers stayed on the job a lot longer than they should have. They were no longer physically able to do the job. Some command officers were over seventy years old. When they finally got a decent pension plan and a mandatory retirement age of sixty years old, things turned around.

I remember the first day I worked on the day shift. I was assigned to work with one of the old-time police officers. He acted like I didn't exist. He didn't say a word to me. When our car came in, he got in the driver's side and slid behind the steering wheel. He drove over and picked up a newspaper and then he stopped at a restaurant and got a coffee to go.

Next we went down by the river where he drank his coffee and read his paper. We had only been together thirty minutes, and I learned there were a lot of streets in town named after him and that was "one way." His next stop was a cold storage warehouse. He said, "You wait here," and got out of the cruiser and went into the building.

I had had enough of him. I got out of the car and followed him inside. I couldn't believe what he did next. He picked up two paper sacks and started filling them with fruit and vegetables. When they were full, he took them out and put them in the back seat of the cruiser.

The merchant looked at me and said, "Aren't you going to load up a sack too?"

"No, I'm not."

He said in a raised voice, "I don't believe it. A cop that won't come in and help himself."

I looked at him and said in a louder voice, "I don't believe it."

He said, "What don't you believe?"

I said, "I don't believe I just saw a merchant watch a cop come into his place of business and load up two sacks of his produce and walk out the door without paying for them. I didn't hear him say, 'Pay for it or put it back.' I didn't hear him say, 'Get the hell out of my store and don't come back or I'll call internal affairs and report you.' I didn't hear him say one single thing."

I went out to the cruiser and I told the officer, "I don't operate the way you do." I said he could put the stuff back or I was going to the captain's office. I won't work with a crook.

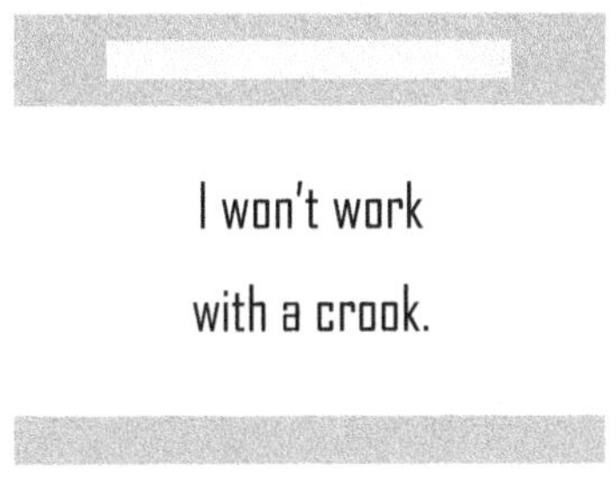

He said, "You're serious?"

"Yes, I am."

He took the sacks back into the market. We never worked together again. He never said another word to me after that, but I really didn't care. He knew he was wrong. He sure didn't want me going to the captain's office.

When the mandatory retirement age became effective, most of these people were forced to retire. Some of the older officers had a hard time adapting to the new ways, but we survived through the transition period and in the end we became one of the finest police departments in the nation. When compared with the other departments, I can honestly say we were head and shoulders above them.

I really enjoyed being on the day shift because I was a part of my family again. My sons and I were able to do many things together for the first time.

Like other families, we did Indian Guides, scouting, softball, football, and swimming. We went fishing and out to the park for weenie roasts. We have a lot of good memories from those days.

I was on the day shift for about a year when they started a traffic warrant section. My old sergeant had called me and asked me to put my name in for it. I was glad that I did. I learned so much about serving warrants and about people in general. It was a good experience for me as well as a challenge.

You must be as crafty as the person you are looking for.

I learned the dos and the don'ts in a hurry while serving traffic warrants. You must be as crafty as the person you are looking for. There are a lot of tricks to the trade. I served thousands of warrants during the time I worked there and never had to fight anyone. I handcuffed everyone I arrested. I enjoyed tracking these people down and seeing their different reactions when they were apprehended.

At one time we served court papers: Restraining orders, nonsupport warrants, eviction orders, check warrants, and others. I was so pleased when our new Chief of Police said we were no longer going to serve these papers because it was the duty of the sheriff's office to do it and not the police department.

But when we were serving papers, we would meet the court bailiff at the location of the eviction. Most of the time the property would be vacated before the paper was served, and the utilities had been shut off for some time. Yet some of the people would continue to stay in the house.

Without water they could not flush the toilet but this did not stop them from using it. When the toilet was full, they used the bathtub, and when that was full, they would move out. The kitchen sink would be full of rotten garbage, and trash would be scattered throughout the whole house.

The worst place I saw was in the late fall of 1967. The utilities had been shut off and it turned cold early that year. The house had a fireplace so the renters not only had burned up the interior doors, woodwork, and kitchen cabinets in the fireplace for heat, they also ripped up the oak floors and burned them before they were evicted. The house was a total loss and the owner had it torn down.

I will always remember serving this restraining order. We received it at our 3:30 p.m. roll call. A note was attached to it that stated, "Must be served between 6:00 p.m. and 6:30 p.m. The party will be there at this time."

We hit out on the radio at 6:10 to serve it. A woman answered the door and we asked for the person named on the order. She asked us to come into the house. She called the man's name and said, "There are two policemen here and they want to talk to you."

He came into the room right away and asked, "Can I help you?"

We explained we had a restraining order for him sworn out by his wife and we served him with his copy. We explained to him if he violated the order, he would be in contempt of court and be subject to arrest.

We told him to give us his house keys and we would escort him while he packed some clothes and got his ditty bag. When we started to leave, we gave her his keys and he said, "Officers, would you look at what she cooked me for supper tonight: prime rib, mashed potatoes, two vegetables, iced tea, and apple pie."

His two children sat there in disbelief with tears in their eyes. He said, "I should have known something was up when she cooked me this meal."

He told his wife he hoped she and her lover have a miserable life, and he told his children he loved them, and we walked outside to his car with him and waited until he left. I didn't like serving orders like these. I was glad when we didn't have to do it anymore.

I didn't mind putting the deadbeats in jail because it was the children they were hurting.

We served so many warrants for nonpayment of child support to the same people, eventually we knew each other by our first names. Some people would not pay their child support until they were forced to. The courts have improved the way they handle the support payments. I didn't mind putting the deadbeats in jail because it was the children they were hurting, but I was still glad when we no longer had to do it. It really is not a police function and it took up so much of our time locating these people, arresting them, and transporting them to jail.

We used to process AWOL (absent without leave) military personal during the Vietnam era. Each branch handled their deserters differently.

The Marine Corps came right down to retrieve their troops when we notified them we had one. I was told they would be in Vietnam in less than two weeks after they left our jail. There weren't many Navy or Air Force personnel. The Marines came down to the jail and picked up the Navy personnel too. They were assigned to sea duty and were restricted to the ship or locked in the brig when they made port. They also had to make up their bad time.

The Air Force and the Army put deserters in the stockade for rehab and gave them a choice of getting out or staying in the service. Most got out.

For reasons unknown, many of their records did not show they were no longer wanted and they were sometimes rearrested and held in our jail until the mistake was corrected. Their records were so far behind that we discontinued picking up military personnel.

Immigration rules and practice changed while I was on the job. At one time when we stopped a vehicle and the people did not speak English or have any identification, we would arrest them and hold them for the immigration authorities who would take it from there.

One day when we came to work we were told that we were no longer going to arrest people who did not speak English or have any identification for the immigration people. Instead we were to write down the name and address these people gave us and send it to immigration, and they would contact the people at the address they gave us.

My partners and I got into a few scuffles over the years.

One partner and I received a disturbance call at this big old house that had been converted into apartments. We entered the front door going into a hallway. My partner was in front of me. A huge black man in his underwear stepped out into the hallway from the first apartment on our right. He didn't say a word. He punched my partner square in the face and my partner went down.

That brief second was all he needed to jerk me up over his head.

I tried to hit the man with my night stick but the end of it caught on the door frame. That brief second was all he needed to jerk me up over his head. Somehow my index finger and middle on my left hand caught in his nose as he raised me over his head. This jerked his head back and I think he fell backward over my partner on the floor.

He hit the floor with the back of his head. I still had my fingers in his nose. He was stunned for a moment, which gave me time to shove my fingers as far up his nose as I could get them. I put a scissor hold on his left arm with my legs and locked my arm around his right arm. I thanked Vernon Ekfelt, my wrestling coach when I was a freshman in high school, for teaching me how to do this.

It was my nose hold that got him. I was pulling up on it as hard as I could. I really had it stretched out. He was screaming, "Let go of my nose, man, let go of my nose."

A woman looked out of the apartment door he had come out of. I asked her to call the police and tell them we need help. She slammed the door shut but no help came. I knew I could hold him as long as his nose didn't rip off. I had about a quarter cup of white heads and blood out of his nose in my hand now. I worried about my partner. I could see him lying on his back under the guy's legs.

I didn't dare turn loose of the man's nose. I knew I would have to shoot him if I did because he would have killed me.

My partner started to come around. I told him to call for help. He looked at us and jumped on the guy. He was pounding on the guy like a professional when I said to put the cuffs on him while I hold his nose. My partner said he was all right He didn't remember he had been knocked out.

The man refused to stand up, so we each grabbed a leg and carefully dragged him out to the car in his underwear and hauled him to jail.

While on another disturbance call between a man and his daughter over a meal she had prepared for him, we got into another scuffle. She was a large woman in her middle thirties and he was in his sixties. She was upset to the point where she about ready to lose it.

> She grabbed a butcher knife from the table.

My partner tried to calm her down but it did no good. She directed all of her anger toward him. She was out of control now, and she grabbed a butcher knife from the table. She went straight at my partner thrusting the knife at him. He drew his service revolver and told her to stop or he would shoot her.

I really think that is what she wanted him to do. At this point I don't think she even realized I was in the room anymore. She was slicing the knife back and forth in the air. As she took a step toward him, he stepped back. I was to her side now and less than three feet away from her. I raised up my stick and brought it down on her wrist as hard as I could, The knife flew out of her hand. She screamed and fell down on her knees holding her wrist.

We grabbed her and put her in handcuffs. We confiscated the knife and transported her to the hospital for x-rays. She didn't have any broken bones.

We took her upstairs to the mental ward for an evaluation and put a hold on her for the police department. She didn't know why she had attacked my partner. We were lucky things worked out the way they did for all of us. Both of these cases could have turned out much worse.

It was a hot night and we stopped at a drive-in restaurant for a cool drink. At the same time they brought our order a man walked up to the driver's door of the cruiser. He said to my partner, "You're the SOB that's been screwing my wife."

"You're the SOB that's been screwing my wife."

I looked up then just as he punched my partner in the face and reached into the car and grabbed him punching him several more times. I got out of the car and ran around to help my partner who was now lying on the seat not moving. I pulled out my spring-loaded sap and gave the guy a shot to the head. The blood flew but it didn't faze him. He got me a good one on my right cheek. I hit him with the sap again and the blood flew. I gave him a couple more licks, and he punched me again. I hit him two more times with the sap and he hit me back both times.

This guy was super human. I saw one of our night sticks on the back seat and the window was down. I threw the sap in the car and grabbed the stick and laid it across his head. This got his attention. He didn't hit me back then but he was still on his feet. He didn't go down. I hit him again and this time he went to his knees. I hit him one more time and he went down.

I handcuffed him and was dragging him to the car when a cruiser came flying in the driveway. Someone had finally called the police station. I was sure glad to see them.

They took the suspect to the hospital and my partner and I drove ourselves. We were checked and released with some pain pills. We were really beat up but they held the suspect for observation.

It was past shift change when we arrived at central station. We were told to go into the captain's office. He was talking to someone in his office. He motioned for us to come in.

"That guy do this to you?" he asked.

We said he had. We really looked bad with our bruised and swollen faces.

He told the man in his office, "I want you to take a good look at them and see what that man did to my two officers and you want to complain on them?" The captain said, "I think you better leave now." The man didn't say a word, he just left.

The captain said the man was a cab driver who thought I used too much force before I put the handcuffs on the guy. We put in our overtime slips and went home.

We went to a preliminary hearing on the guy from the drive-in a week later. I never would have recognized him as the person who assaulted us. The doctors had to shave his head so they could stitch up every place where it was split. His head appeared to be swollen and black and blue with some yellow and green mixed in. He had many stitches and lumps.

My partner and I had pictures of the way we looked. He was bound over to the district court for trial and later served time.

My partner was not his wife's lover. Even if he had been, I still could not have stood by and watched him being assaulted. I did what I had to do. I will never know if his wife was having an extramarital with a police officer or if the bad guy had some kind of a mental problem. Since his record doesn't show any further contacts with the police after that, I think he may have had marital problems.

If we had Tasers like they have today, I never would have had to slug it out with him. The first thing I did with my sap after that was to throw it in the trash. The only thing it was good for was to make someone mad and get you hurt.

> If we had Tasers like they have today, I never would have had to slug it out with him.

If I had only taken my stick with me when I got out of the car instead of relying on the sap, the fight would have been over a lot sooner and I might not have had to take such a beating.

- Eight -

STREET STORIES, PROWLERS, AND VOYEURS

During my years on the police department I only witnessed two cases of voyeurism. One was a man on the porch of a house with his face pressed against the glass in the front window watching a young woman dancing inside. He was so excited by what he was seeing, he didn't know we were standing beside him.

The second time I stopped the cruiser behind a big fancy luxury car parked next to a building and walked up to it. I observed an obese older man sitting in the back seat. He was leaning forward over the back of the front seat looking down at something on the front seat.

I turned my flashlight on his face; sweat was pouring out of his forehead and running down his face and dripping off his chin. He was in a different world. His mouth was open and he was panting like a dog. He didn't see my light or even know I was there.

I shined my light on the front seat and saw a nude couple having sex.

I shined my light on the front seat and saw a nude couple having sex. They jumped up and started putting their clothes on. They were both teenagers—he was sixteen and she was fifteen. The man in the backseat had paid them to have sex so he could watch. I called for a backup and we took all of them down to the station. I wanted to go to court on this creep, but I never had the chance. He pled guilty at his arraignment and I was never notified.

We received numerous calls of prowlers and voyeurs (Peeping Toms) at one address where a comely teenage girl lived. Her father thought it might be their neighbor, but it could have been anyone who had ever seen her. I told them they had to keep her shades pulled.

I went next door to talk to the neighbor, a man in his early thirties. He said he had heard they were having problems but he had never seen anything. We talked for a while and then I told him I was getting tired of making the calls there.

I said, "I think I'll go back over there and tell him if it were me and I heard something outside by my window, I would shoot through the screen and ask questions later."

I went back to the victim's house and told them I would check their house more often. I never had another call there. The father may have been correct in thinking it might be their neighbor.

One afternoon, we had a little more than one inch of fresh snow, and it turned cold later that night. We received a call of a prowler around 8:30 p.m. The woman who called said she had taken a shower and was putting on her nightgown so she could read a book and relax before she went to bed. She said she had this feeling as if someone was watching her. She noticed her blinds were not closed all the way, and she saw a man with his face pressed against the screen looking in.

She saw a man with his face pressed against the screen.

She said it scared her, but she walked out of the room and pretended like nothing happened and called 911. We went outside and checked where she said the man was standing by the window. There were perfect shoeprints in the fresh snow. We could see where he walked up to the window and put his gloved hands in the snow on the window ledge while he looked into the house. There were shoeprints leading out to the front sidewalk. We followed the shoeprints for over half a block before they turned up to a house with an enclosed front porch.

We rang the doorbell and the porch light came on. There in plain view sitting in a boot tray by the door were the wet rubber boots that made the footprints. A teenage boy in stocking feet had answered the door.

"I want to look at your boots," I said.

He picked up the boots and showed them to me. There was no doubt they were the ones that made the footprints. His mother came to the door and asked what the problem was.

I said, "It looks like we have a problem," and told her the whole story.

She said, "There must be some kind of a mistake."

No mistake, I said. "I would like you to put on your hat and coat and come with us so you can see for yourself."

I asked her how old her son was, and she said fifteen.

I picked up one of the boots and we showed her his boot was the same as the prints left in the snow. We back-tracked them to the window where he looked into the neighbor's house, and I showed her where her son first walked up to the window. I put the boot in the snow several times while we were walking so she would know they matched.

"I don't know what to say," she said, convinced. "It is so hard to believe."

"Family is always the last to know when something like this happens," I told her. "Your son is young. They may be able to help him. We're going to take your son to the youth bureau and he will go to juvenile court. You be there when he does and get him in a program for kids with his problem."

She said she would.

I was driving through the park one morning when I noticed a car off the roadway parked on the grass next to the swimming pool. It was a strange place to leave a car. I checked it out. The doors were locked, the ignition switch appeared to be intact. There was no stolen report on it.

Later in the morning I received a call to take the report of a stolen auto three blocks away from the swimming pool. It turned out to be the same car I checked in the park by the swimming pool. When we went to the park to recover the car, it started right up with the keys the owner gave us.

Since there were no signs of a forced entry or any damage to the car, I asked the owner if she had a spare key hidden on the car. Yes, in a hide-a-key box. I asked her to check it and discovered it was gone.

I made out a stolen vehicle report and a recovered vehicle report. I advised her to have the locks changed if she didn't want them to take her car again. We were having a number of cars stolen for parts at that time. They were dumping the carcass of the cars in the different secluded areas of the city under the cover of darkness and setting them on fire early in the morning. With each fire it was as if the thieves were thumbing their noses at the police department. We finally learned from a good source where the chop shop was located.

We advised the auto theft unit, and one night they were able to catch the thieves stripping a stolen car. After this shop was shut down, we didn't have any stripped cars set on fire in our district. We still had cars stolen that were never recovered, but they could have been taken out of the state or even the country as far as that goes. The cars taken for joy riding were still being recovered locally.

When the car alarms first came out, vehicle owners thought they were going to be a deterrent to autos being stolen. People are so used to the alarms going off now, they don't even look when one does. Someday an anti-theft device will be developed that can't be compromised.

But until then, as long as there are automobiles, there will be someone who will want to steal it.

One week I arrested two parties for exposing themselves. One was a large thirteen-year-old boy who was mentally challenged. He really didn't know he was doing anything wrong when he had to go to the bathroom and some children saw him.

> Exposed himself twice to a young woman waiting at a bus stop.

The other one had exposed himself twice to a young woman waiting at a bus stop on her way to work. She gave a good description of him and his car but didn't get his license number. It happened at the same time on two days. I thought I would give the area a little special attention the next day and see if the car came by again.

He came by. I stopped the car and the driver fit the description of the wanted party. We talked for a while and I told him I knew what he did and I knew why he did it. I was gaining his trust.

We talked some more and he confessed to exposing himself to the woman on both nights. He said he really scared her, and it felt good when he did it. I took him down to the detective bureau. The man in charge that night was one of those people who gave everyone a hard time because he could get away with it.

He wanted to know why I brought the party in. I said, "I brought him in because he is wanted for exposing himself to a woman at the bus stop."

He said, "You don't know that."

"He told me he did it."

The detective looked over my report and told me to take the suspect down to the jail and book him.

I said, "Thank you, sir, I will do that. You have a nice day."

"Are you trying to be smart?" he accused me.

I looked at him and said, "Why would I do that?" and walked out of his office.

After I booked the suspect I got in my cruiser and drove back to my district. I thought how fortunate I was not to be working in the detective bureau. The man's wife had recently divorced him and I could see why. He had to be a lonely person.

- Nine -

ALL IN THE FAMILY—DISTURBANCES, DOMESTIC VIOLENCE, AND COLD SPAGHETTI

We saw our share of family problems played out in beatings and violence. Here are some of the horrors we found when called to the scene—and how our fellow citizens addressed their domestic problems.

I received a radio call around 7:30 p.m. to back up another officer on a family disturbance call. I met him about a block away from the house, and we went in on the call together. The woman was a mental case, but her husband would not commit her. Their ten-year-old son had called police this time. When she took her medication, she was all right, but she would not always take it as she should.

The father said she had taken a pill and would calm down in a bit. We tried to get him to let us take her to the hospital, and he could follow us but he refused. She eventually started to calm down. There was nothing we could do, so we left.

Twenty minutes later we were back at the house. She had shot and killed him with his shotgun. Her sister was there now, and she was taking the boy to her house. A detective arrived and we transported the woman to the mental ward.

She had shot and killed him with his shotgun.

I worked this district for a year before I put my name in to transfer to the day shift. One night in 1962 shortly before I went to the day shift, I had a new officer with me when we received a shooting call. The rescue squad was en route but we arrived on the call before they did.

The house was a small, well-maintained older home. An elderly woman who appeared to be in her eighties answered the door. I asked, "Did you call us, Ma'am?"

She said, "Yes. Come in."

When she turned I saw the shooting victim in the next room. He was sitting in a chair at the dining room table. He had fallen forward head first onto the table. His arms were positioned as if he tried to break his fall. His face was buried in a plate of spaghetti. A glass of ice water on the table next to the plate had not been disturbed.

A small black-and-white portable television set on the table across from him was turned on. A large part of the back of his head now covered the wall across the room.

She said, "I was tired of my husband not coming home for supper."

She would cook him a good meal and it just sat there and got cold. Then she would have to throw it out. She told him time after time when supper would be ready, but it didn't do any good, she told us. He would go down to the corner to sit and talk with his old cronies and forget about the time.

> His face was buried in a plate of spaghetti.

He came home late again that night, so she put the cold food on the table. He sat down to eat it and turned the TV on but didn't say a word to her. She said she had enough of him and went into the bedroom and got the shotgun.

He was eating the cold spaghetti and watching the TV when she walked up behind him, raised the shotgun, pointed it at the back of his head, and pulled the trigger. She had put the shotgun away and called the police.

The rescue squad came and took the body to the county hospital where an autopsy would be done in the morning. The detective bureau advised us to bring her in. She had no family. We made our reports and confiscated the shotgun and the spent shell. We made sure the house was locked and took her to the detective bureau. We turned her over to them. I don't know what happened to her.

One woman called the police on her husband almost every Friday evening. When he got off work on Friday, he would stop on his way home and pick up a case of beer. He drove for a living and he didn't dare get arrested for DUI because he would lose his job. He never drank at a bar or when he had to drive. He would bring the beer home though and drink it all at one sitting. Then the fighting would begin.

He never hit her but the yelling and screaming was unbelievable. The children went outside when they couldn't take it anymore. She refused to have him put in jail because it cost them money, which they needed to feed their children. They had thirteen kids.

She had him arrested once, but it only made things worse because it cost them money they didn't have and he continued to drink anyway. He knew she wouldn't have him arrested and things got worse. He started to drink on other nights in addition to the Friday nights. The children's lives were now being affected.

Someone must have called the child protection agency because they lost their children. We quit getting calls there. He quit drinking and their fighting stopped. I don't know if they ever got all of their children back, but we did see children at the house at different times.

We had another weekly caller—an older man who rode the bus home from work, but he got off the bus at the neighborhood bar about two blocks from his home where he got loaded before he walked on home and fought with his wife. She would have him arrested and put in jail every time. He finally got the message and quit his drinking. We never made any more calls there.

He was bleeding from a cut on his chest and a stab wound on his upper arm.

We went out on a call about a cutting one night. The man who answered the door was the person who called. He was bleeding from a cut on his chest and a stab wound on his upper arm. He said his wife did it. They had been talking while they were eating supper when she flew into a rage for no reason and grabbed her steak knife and cut him. She ran into the bedroom.

He didn't know what to do so he called 911. He said she was still in the bedroom. We asked her to come out so we could talk to her. When she came out of the room, she saw him and said, "You're hurt. I'll get some bandages," and she left the room.

She came back with some gauze, a roll of tape, and a pair of small scissors and started to bandage his wounds. Suddenly she was a different person with a different voice. She said, "I'll kill you, you SOB," and she tried to stab him with the scissors.

My partner and I grabbed her. She was super strong but we got her handcuffed. She was in a wild rage, so we took both of them to the hospital.

While en route to the hospital, she came out of her rage and asked where we were going. Yet she went back into the rage while we were in the emergency room when the doctor was checking her husband.

The doctor said, "I've studied this illness but I have never witnessed it before." The doctor told us to take her up to the fifth floor (the mental ward) and they would take care of her. They were waiting for us there.

We took the handcuffs off and they put their restraining devices on her before they took her through the locked doors. We went back to the emergency room. The husband was stitched up and we made our reports. The woman had some type of mental breakdown where she became two different people. We took her husband home and wished the best for him.

> She had whacked him several more times on the head.

One Sunday afternoon, we were patrolling through the housing projects when a man ran out the front door of one of the units with a woman right behind him. She had a claw hammer in her hand, and she hit him on the head with it and he went down. We stopped as quickly as we could, but before we could stop her, she had whacked him several more times on the head. He was bleeding profusely but was still conscious. They both had had too much to drink.

We called the rescue squad for him.

He kept saying, “That woman must really love me the way she pounded on my head.”

The squad took him to the county hospital and we took her to the city jail for assault with a weapon. We were at the hospital later, and I asked how the man was who was hit on the head with the hammer was doing. They said the x-rays didn’t show anything and he didn’t have any concussions, so they stitched him up and sent him home. They said he had one thick skull.

We received a call of a shooting at the bar next to the projects. When we got there, they said no one had called and there was no shooting there. I knew one man sitting at the bar, so I asked him if he saw anything.

No, he said, he had just gotten there. We talked for a minute and left. Two hours later we received a call in the projects to see a party about the shooting call we had in the bar. The caller was the man who had been sitting at the bar.

"Why'd you call us now?" I asked.

"I have to go to the hospital," he said. "I got shot in the bar."

"Why didn't you say anything when I asked you at the bar?"

"I was too scared," he said.

I told him to show me where he was hit. He took a small round in his abdomen on the lower left and it passed through him and came out of his back.

I said, "I wish you would have told us you were shot sooner. I don't know if you will make it now."

"What do you mean you don't know if I'll make it?"

I said, "Infection. You better tell me what happened so we will have a record of who shot you."

He told me everything and I made the report. I also made a bar report on the owner of the bar. He lied to me when he said no one was shot in his bar. He would have to explain why he lied when he comes up for his license renewal.

We transported our shooting victim to the hospital where he was about to undergo a surgical procedure he would never forget.

I remember one unusual disturbance call. Three people were involved in it: one woman and two men. They lived in an apartment on the first floor of a huge older two-and-a-half-story home that had been converted into four apartments. One of the men owned the house. The three of them shared the apartment. The other man paid him half as much as he charged the other people for their apartments, and they split the grocery bill. They both paid the woman to clean the apartment, cook, do their laundry, and be their aid.

"She is our sex aid."

I had to ask what their aid was for. He said, "She is our sex aid and that is the problem. I'm supposed to have her on Tuesdays and Thursdays. He has her on Wednesdays and Fridays. She has Saturdays, Sundays, and Mondays off. When I came home from work today, I found them in bed together and this is Thursday. My day and not his. They said they thought it was Friday."

I had heard everything now. I said, "Since you own the house, you can put him out or you can put her out or you can put them both out. Or you could buy a yellow highlighter pen and he could buy a red one and mark your days in yellow and he can mark his in red. This way there shouldn't be any more problems."

They thought it was a good idea. It must have been because we never had another call from them.

We had a call from a woman who said her husband was sneaking her clothing out of her closet and wearing them when he went out on the town in drag. She found out about this practice when she had to bond him out of jail and he was wearing her clothing.

She wasn't happy with him at all, but she said she wasn't going to harm him. She was just mad at him for wearing her clothes. She knew he liked to wear women's clothing but he could buy his own. She liked the lifestyle he provided for her, and she wasn't about to give it up.

It looked as if we weren't needed there, so we left.

We received a radio call of a disturbance at 7:45 one morning. We seldom had a disturbance call this early.

When we arrived on the call, a man answered the door. We asked him if he called and he said no it was probably his sister, and he called out a woman's name. He then stepped out past us onto the front stoop. A woman then came to the door and yelled, "That's him, that's him."

"That's him" was now running full bore down the street. I started to give chase but when I stepped on the grass it was wet and I slipped and fell. The guy was about a half block down the street by now when his after-burners kicked in and he was gone.

The woman said she woke up when she heard her brother talking to someone. She said she looked out and saw who it was. She put on her robe and told him to get out of her house because she had called the police. She didn't want any criminals in her house. She gave us his name and said he had escaped from the state prison three months earlier and different people had been hiding him in their homes since then. We didn't know anything about a prison break.

He had walked away from a work detail. We didn't know about the escapee because it happened on our days off. We made an information report on today's sighting of him.

The prison workout area with its weights and other exercise equipment had served him well. He was one big bad dude now. A lot of the younger people looked up to him as a hero figure because he was defying authority, and some of the older people were afraid of him. Whatever their reasons were, there had been enough people to feed and hide him for the last three months.

Whoever apprehended this party was going to have their hands full. He wasn't going to go without a fight. We saw him on the street corner several days later, but he was gone before we could stop. This guy was starting to make us look bad.

My partner and I discussed the best way to take this guy. We agreed that we had to get him off his feet right away. If we didn't, we were going to get hurt. We had mace now. We would try it first. Once we had him cuffed we could handle him. We found out real soon after that how good our plan was.

We received information on where the escapee was hiding. We called for backup because we knew he was a jack rabbit and he would run. We were going to watch the house until backup got there to help us. It was a corner house. My partner covered the front and I covered the back. We stood where we could see each other. We were not going to attempt to make contact with him until our backup was in place. Our friend in the house had other plans. He must have known we had help on the way. If he was going to escape, he decided he'd better do it now.

He charged out of the front door like a raging bull running straight at my partner.

He charged out of the front door like a raging bull running straight at my partner. My partner held his ground as he yelled for me. Just like the mace directions said, he sprayed it on the man's chest and neck. It slowed him down, but he was still able to pick my partner up off the ground. I hit the man as hard as I could with my stick on the back of his knee causing him to go down. We were on top of him now. My partner gave him another shot of mace, but it didn't seem to bother him. It sure got us.

We finally managed to get the handcuffs on him. The tear gas was killing us. Someone said "good job guys." Our backup had arrived. Neither of us had been sprayed with the mace. It was just the fumes coming off our arrest that got us. They didn't seem to be bothering him.

We washed off with someone's garden hose and it helped. We had our backup take the arrest into the station while we recovered. We took our shirts off and drove to a gas station where we washed with soap and water. It took quite a while for the smell to leave our clothing. Our backup team had to stop and get out of their car on the way to the station when the gas got to them. We had to laugh at them over that.

We never tried using our mace after that. I understand the pepper spray they use now is much better. I did manage to get mace on me one more time when my canister got a hole in it from rubbing on its holster.

The deputy chief in charge of the police property wanted me to come into his office when I came on duty. He was known to be a cantankerous person. He wanted to see my mace container. I gave it to him and showed him where it leaked out. He wanted to know how I knew it was leaking. I said I smelled it and my eyes started to burn. I could see where a mist was spraying out and hear it hissing. He wanted to know how I knew it was empty. I said I put the canister on the ground and left it there until it quit spraying. I just assumed it was empty.

I said, "Give it to me and I'll see if it's empty."

He asked me what I was going to do. I said I'm going to see if it will spray.

"No, don't. That won't be necessary," he told me. "Go down to the property room and tell them that I said to give you a new one."

I said, "Thank you, sir. I'll do that."

I don't know why the man acted the way he did. I guess he just had to. I went down to the property room and picked up a new canister, which I never used.

I was working a two-man car when we received a call one afternoon to see a party about trespassers. We seldom had a call in that area. When we arrived on the call, a man said when his children went out to play on their swing set, they came right back into the house and told him a man and a woman with no clothes on were lying on a blanket in their yard.

He said he went outside to see for himself, and there they were in plain view not forty feet away his house having sex on a blanket in his yard. He said it made him so mad he thought he'd better call us rather than try to talk to them himself.

We went around the house and, sure enough, a nude couple were lying on a blanket sleeping. We recognized the man. He was a derelict from the skid row section on the eastern edge of the downtown area. We had arrested him numerous times for public drunkenness. We didn't know who the woman was. We had never seen her before.

We were trying to wake her when the man woke up. He was still very drunk. He had a hard time trying to get his clothes on, but neither of us volunteered to help him. We asked him what he was doing there, and he said, "Getting laid."

I said, "We can see that, but where did you meet her?"

He said she picked him up on the street and wanted to know if he wanted to party. He said he would like to but he didn't have any money. She told him, "You don't need any money, just get in the car."

He got in and they went to a couple of bars and then she bought a bottle and drove out to this home. I asked where they left the car, and he said he didn't know. My partner finally got the woman to wake up.

She was indignant. "Do you know who I am?"

She was indignant. "Do you know who I am?"

We didn't.

She said, "I'm the mayor's wife, and I'm going to have your jobs."

My partner said, "I know the mayor's wife and you're not her."

She said mayor so and so will hear about this. My partner said you can tell him when he gets you out of jail. We heard later that there was a mayor with the name she said in one of the smaller towns close by us, but we don't know or care if they were related.

The woman refused to put her clothes on and started to become combative. We put handcuffs on her and put both of them into the cruiser. She went in the back seat with my partner. I put the blanket over her, and her boyfriend rode in the front with me. She calmed down by the time we reached the police station.

We had a female officer meet us at the jail, and she took the woman into one of the interrogation rooms to retrieve my handcuffs and have the woman put her clothes on. We booked her and her boyfriend for public drunkenness, disorderly conduct, indecent exposure, and trespassing.

We never went to court on either of them so they must have pled guilty. We never knew what happened to her car.

I met a lot of strange people being a police officer, but one of the strangest ones was on a domestic violence call. This woman wanted us to stand by while she packed some clothes. She said she had had enough of her husband's abuse and kinky behavior. She was getting out.

He was begging her to stay. He said he would get some help. She said there was no way she was going to stay. She put up with his sickness far too long. He was always going to get help but he never did and she knew he never would.

She said, "I'll show you what he brought home today."

"Please don't do that," he told her.

She went into another room while he left the house through the front door.

She came back with a cardboard carton and said her husband had brought this home today. It was his latest sex toy and he planned on using it on her that night. She took it out of the box and held it up saying it's called the destroyer.

It was his latest sex toy and he planned on using it on her that night.

It was a large vinyl dildo, over a foot long, an inch and a half in diameter, with a crank at its base. When she turned the crank, this thing did all sorts of gyrations and inward and outward motions.

She said, "Do you want to see some more of his perverted stuff?"

We said, "No. Get your bag. We have to go."

Her husband never came back while we were there.

- Ten -

THE SUMMER OF LOVE AND RIOTS, AND I END UP IN JAIL

I served warrants for two years and then went back to the cruiser patrol in the summer of 1966 during the time of the civil unrest or race riots as they were called. I worked the day shift from 6:00 a.m. to 6:00 p.m. All summer vacations were canceled so I planned a winter camping trip with my boys.

We had a pop-up camper with hard walls and it was self-contained. When the boys had their Christmas vacation in 1968, the boys and I took five days and camped at the Fremont Lakes. We had the whole place to ourselves. The lakes were frozen and they were posted with signs stating they had poisoned the fish in the lake, but we didn't care. We could not have fished if we had wanted to since the lakes were frozen over with eighteen inches of ice.

My one son brought his bow with some arrows and we all had our bikes. We had a good time except for one afternoon when my twelve-year-old was outside shooting arrows at a cardboard box while the rest of us were inside the camper watching television. There was a knock at the door. A man was there with my son in tow and he had my son's bow.

"Is this your son?" he asked.

I said yes. He said he was bow fishing, and he can't bow fish in this lake.

"Who are you?" I asked.

He showed me a badge that said Nebraska Game Warden. I thought he must have been new because he was very nervous. I asked how my son could have been bow fishing on a lake that is covered with a foot of ice and posted with signs that say there are no fish in it.

He said, "You can't have a bow in the park."

I said I didn't know that. I told him I would put it away and we would never bring it to the park again.

"Let this be a warning to you," he said as he left.

I thought to myself the kids will remember this vacation for sure now.

That evening there was another knock on the door, and I thought now what. It was a woman who ran out of gas on the highway by the park. She saw our trailer and wanted to know if I could help her. I said I would take her to a gas station.

I loaded her and the boys into our station wagon and went down the highway to a gas station where she bought some gas. I took her back to her car and helped her get it started. When we got home, I thought one of the boys would tell their mother about the game warden.

But the first thing my number three son said when we walked in the house was, "Dad, did you tell Mom about the lady that was in the camper?"

My wife looked at me and said, "You are going to tell Mom about the lady that was in the camper, aren't you." I told her about the woman and the game warden. She said, "It really sounds like you had a good time."

Spring came and like so many other cities that year we had our sit-ins at the local university. I was a student there at that time and wondered if a student might recognize me as we carried them out of the president's office to the awaiting paddy wagons in step with their singing of "We Shall Overcome."

We also had our hippie movement, the underground press, the concerts in the parks, and the Vietnam War protests. Yes, we had it all and I was there to see most of it. I remember when the Old Market area closed down and the hippie squatters moved in and started their little shops in the vacant buildings. The hippies taking over the Old Market were the beginning of what we see there today in the boutiques and shops. That's how it all started.

The hippies taking over the Old Market were the beginning of what we see there today in the boutiques and shops.

Buildings were burned during the race riots, and I had to leave the area because my car was low on fuel. I dared not run out of fuel there for fear they would burn the car and harm me. En route to get fuel, I was stopped by a young woman who said her mother was in her car, and she thought she was having a heart attack. I called for a rescue squad and removed the woman from the car and started CPR.

A car stopped and a black woman got out and walked over to me and said, "I know CPR. I can help you." I let her take over because she was better at CPR than I was, and I assisted her until the squad arrived.

Ironically, two miles away the police were being stoned by some blacks and here this black woman was helping me, a white officer, trying to save a white woman's life. I never got her name, but I will never forget her.

The riotous summer ended and things began to slow down until the holidays came and the town went wild. Five people were dead one weekend. My partner and I worked two of the cases. One was a cutting and the other one came out as a "make an investigation," which normally means a natural death.

The cutting was a domestic violence call in which the woman stabbed her husband in the stomach just below the sternum with a wooden-handled carving knife. Only the handle was sticking out of him when we found him sitting on a couch in his living room. He had a large beer belly on him, and the knife appeared to be stuck in him going downward at a 45-degree angle.

"What happened?" I asked him.

"My wife did it," he told me.

His wife was in the kitchen doing the dishes and talking to my partner. He was trying to get her side of the story. She said he beat her badly once before, and she wasn't going to let him do it again. She said he hadn't liked the way she was cooking their dinner, and he came in the kitchen yelling at her.

She knew he was going to hit her, so she grabbed the carving knife off the counter. When he grabbed her, she stabbed him as hard as she could. She said he let go of her and looked at the knife handle. He cupped his hands holding his stomach below the knife as he turned and walked slowly back into the living room where he sat down on the couch. She called the rescue squad.

Her husband was DOA (dead on arrival) at the hospital.

We took her to the detective bureau and gave our reports to the captain on duty. He looked them over and had us put her in the holding cell for the detective who was going to do the follow-up investigation.

The following day we had a "make an investigation" case. When we arrived on the call, a man was sitting on the front steps with his head hanging down. He was holding it up with a hand on each side of his face.

"Did you call us?" I asked.

He mumbled something, stood up, opened the storm door, and held it for us while he opened the front door, and we all went into the house with him. We followed him down a hallway to the last door on our left. He opened the door and stepped back.

I expected to see a deceased person in a bed. I did not expect to see what I saw.

Lying on the floor in a one-inch-thick mixture of blood and water was the body of a dead woman. Her only clothing was a half-slip, which was pulled up over her hips. She was lying on her back with her arms extended almost straight out from her body.

I noticed the toes on her left foot were twisted around the leg of an end table, which indicated that the body had been rolled over. Most of her hair had been pulled

Two small children were in the room with her—covered with blood.

out by its roots, and her face appeared to have been beaten. Her hair lay in piles on the floor about her head.

Two small children were in the room with her—covered with blood. They had been drawing on the walls with their hands using their mother's blood.

"What happened?" I asked.

"I killed her."

I didn't say anything more to him. I phoned radio and told them what we had and asked for the homicide unit to come out and gave them the phone number where we could be reached. I also asked radio to send the crime lab and the juvenile officers out for the children.

We made our original reports and gave them to the detectives when they arrived. They talked to the suspect and took him to the police station. We waited for the crime lab to finish their investigation. Juvenile took the children and the county coroner had the body removed.

We learned later that the suspect had come home and caught her in bed with his friend who lived with them. He jumped on both of them, but the friend managed to get away by jumping out the window. Someone had brought the friend to the station without any clothing on. He told the people in the detective bureau he knew the man would kill her, so they had sent a cruiser out to the house to make an investigation.

We had a water skiing accident at the lake one afternoon in the summer of 1969. A woman was water skiing and her boyfriend was operating the boat. She fell and somehow became tangled in the ski rope. He didn't see her right away. She took a beating and almost drowned by the time he did.

She had to be taken to the hospital by the rescue squad. We made the report and I always wondered how she explained her injuries to her husband when he came home from work that day.

In 1970, I received a call to go into the mayor's office at City Hall. This was rather strange because several police officers were there. They said they were going to take a group picture of the people who were getting promoted. This was news to me. They lined us up and took our pictures and told us what our assignments were.

I was going to the "C" shift traffic section. I had a week to get my uniforms in order before I was promoted.

Three days later we got a call to come into the inspector's office. We looked at each other and wondered what we did now. It was March 27, 1970. He said I was being promoted and gave me my sergeant's badge and hat shield. He said I would be working days for the next ten days before I went to the "C" shift. I was able to get a uniform put together that day.

When we reported back in service, my partner said, "One sergeant and one patrolman." A lot of officers clicked their radio mics then. They gave me a proper send off. I picked up my uniform that afternoon and everything worked out fine.

- Eleven -

TRAGIC ACCIDENTS

I liked the "C" shift and working in the traffic section was like getting a bonus. I thought I would have to work the midnight shift when I was promoted since one loses all of his seniority when moving to a higher rank. Because I was promoted early, that moved me up on the seniority list.

I was driving westbound on the Interstate in a 60 mph zone in my marked cruiser when a car flew past me. I clocked him at 85 mph. When I turned on my red lights and tapped the siren, he pulled right over. I advised radio of my traffic stop and my location. I walked up to the stopped car and asked him for his operator's license, registration, and proof of insurance. Once I had the items, I advised the driver that he was clocked going 85 in a 60 zone and I was going to write him a ticket.

I explained the ticket to him and showed him where he had to sign it.

"You can't give me a ticket unless you have a Smokey the Bear hat."

He told me, "You can't give me a ticket unless you have a Smokey the Bear hat. This is a federal highway and out of your jurisdiction."

"Where did you hear that?" I asked.

"I'm a law student."

"I don't think you heard right," I said and asked him again if he was going to sign the ticket.

When he replied he wasn't, I called for a tow truck and a traffic car. I arrested him and towed his car in for safekeeping.

He must have talked with someone smarter before coming to court because he pleaded guilty.

I recall one large music concert the traffic crew worked in one of our larger parks in the city during the summer of 1972. It was a sellout. The gates to Dodge Park had to be closed so no one else could enter.

Shortly after the concert started, we could detect the smell of marijuana in the air and it got stronger as the night wore on. When the concert was getting near the end, the crowd was getting pretty wild. Most of the police officers had to leave so they could direct the traffic leaving the park when it was over.

The fans didn't want the band to stop playing and they were becoming a little more than upset. Things were about to get out of hand when the power suddenly went off, plunging the park into pitch darkness.

Twenty minutes later the crowd was about gone. The park manager said he didn't think they would have any more concerts there. It was just too much of an overload on their electrical system. He was right. They never had another concert there. I often wondered where he was when the lights went out and why he seemed to grin when he said they overloaded the circuits.

Personal injury calls were part of my work in the traffic division. Cars crash into other cars, into stationary objects, and all kinds of vehicles crash into each other.

I received a call of a boating accident on our local lake. A small boat with an oversized engine crashed into a larger sailboat and went over the top of it. In doing so the prop on the engine of the small boat sliced through the right foot and leg of the passenger in the sailboat. All five of his toes were almost severed. Only the skin on the sole of his foot held them together.

A second laceration went through the instep, and again this part of his foot was only held on by the skin under his foot. A third cut went through the ankle and almost severed his foot. Only the tendons on his heel were keeping the mangled foot from falling off.

I was trying to get all of his information before the rescue squad arrived so I wouldn't have to drive all the way to the hospital to complete my report. I got his name and asked him his address. Turns out he lived next door to my parents. I looked at him and then I recognized him. I had known him for years and still talked to him off and on. He was in such a state of shock that I hadn't recognized him and he didn't know me.

The squad arrived. Someone had put a tourniquet on his leg. They left it alone and put a splint on his foot and ankle. They loaded him in the squad and transported him to the hospital. His older brother whom I did not know at the time was on the sailboat with him. I made sure everyone involved in the accident had the information they needed and told them how to get a copy of the police report.

I saw the young man with the injured leg some time later when I was visiting my parents. He said he lost his leg below the knee, but he was getting around well on his new leg. He didn't remember talking to me at the accident.

I also went on a personal injury accident involving a motorcycle and a semi-tractor trailer truck. I realized later that I knew the deceased man on the motorcycle. We had attended some classes together at the university.

The rider was wearing his helmet, but it was of no help when the dual tires on the tractor ran over his head.

The truck had made a left turn in front of the motorcycle. The rider was wearing his helmet, but it was of no help when the dual tires on the tractor ran over his head. One of our accident investigators made out the report. I directed traffic and waited for the tow truck to pick up the motorcycle. I never recognized the motorcycle rider at the scene. He was no longer identifiable because his head was crushed so badly.

When I went to school the following morning, the class was all talking about him being killed on his motorcycle by a truck that turned in front of him. I realized then who the motorcycle rider was and a chill came over me. I never said anything about being at the accident.

School was the University of Omaha (later University of Nebraska-Omaha), which was offering a bachelor of science degree in criminal justice. A friend that I worked with had said we should look into going to school. The city would pay for some of it, and it might become a requirement for promotion in the future.

I thought why not. I still had my GI Bill, plus a grant that paid for books and tuition as long as I maintained a certain grade point average and stayed in law enforcement for two years following the completion of my last class. I was able to test out of some classes and received credit for my military service. I never talked to the city about their program. I got everything together and in the fall of 1967 became a part-time student. I soon discovered that my grades were much better in college than they had been in high school.

Perhaps I had my mind on other things while I was in high school.

Two years after my college graduation, my obligation to the federal grant was fulfilled, and I had my degree in criminal justice free and clear.

Only a few of the students in my classes knew I was a cop. Most of them assumed I was in the military because I sat with many former military people in the cafeteria. I never told anyone I wasn't one of them. I met a lot of good young people when I went to college and most of them rose to the top of the different fields they chose to go into. I'm sure the young man who was killed on his motorcycle was one who would have made it to the top if he had gotten the chance.

Another unusual situation was a drowning call on the river at the Omaha docks where they load and offload the barges. The deck hands were offloading a barge when three of them were accidently knocked into the river. They had their life jackets on, but they had been caught in the undertow caused by the barge tied up to the dock down river from them. They were pulled under.

The river boat captain explained the way the front end of the barges are designed causes a down current following down the front of the barge and a swirling effect before it goes under the barge.

He said their bodies would be held there in the swirling water until the barge was no longer facing into the current, and there was no way to get them out until they moved the barge. He said since the deck hands had life jackets on, they should pop right out of the water once the barge turned to go up the river. He said they would call us when they were ready to move the barges. I made my reports and left.

Suddenly pop, pop, pop, the bodies shot up out of the water.

I was off the next two days, but my relief said it went like clockwork. The fire and rescue people were waiting downstream in their boat. The riverboat captain hit his throttle and started to nose the barges out into the river.

Suddenly pop, pop, pop, the bodies shot up out of the water just like the river boat captain said they would, and the fire and rescue people were ready. They hooked the bodies and tied ropes to them so they could tow them out of the river.

I was glad it was my day off. I've seen drowning victims before, and they aren't the most pleasant to see. For the sake of their families I was pleased the recovery of the bodies went so well.

One morning before 8:00 a.m. we hit in service on the radio and they gave us a call of a hit-and-run personal injury accident. There were two vehicles in the intersection. One car was smashed into the driver's side of the other car. This car had a stop sign and the car hit in the side was on a through street and had the right of way.

The driver of the car with the stop sign had gotten out of his car and ran down the street and turned at the corner. He was described as a light-skinned black male twenty years old, 5 feet 10 inches, 170 pounds, large afro haircut, wearing a green pullover golf shirt, tan pants and white shoes. The driver of the second car said she could drive her car and she would go to her own doctor. We made the report and towed the other car in.

We reported back in service and radio gave us a call to obtain the report of a stolen auto. When we arrived on the call, a light-skinned black male with a large afro walked out to our car. He was wearing a green pullover shirt, tan pants, and white shoes. My partner said, "Well would you look at that?"

The man said he came out to go to work and his car was gone. He said he parked it there last night at 9:00 p.m. and locked it up. We asked him to have a seat in the rear of the squad car and we would make a report. He got in and I turned the rear view mirror so he could see in it.

I asked him, "Can you tell me how your hair got so full of little pieces of glass?"

He looked in the mirror and tried to brush it out. I told him to stop. I didn't want the glass in my car. I asked him if he realized he could go to jail for making a false police report. He didn't say anything.

"We're going to take you down for a line-up and have the people pick you out as the driver of your car when it was involved in a personal injury accident and you ran away from a personal injury accident. You're looking at some big time," I said.

"I don't want to make a stolen car report."

I asked him why he left when the woman was hurt.

He said, "I was scared and I didn't know she was hurt."

We took him down to the accident office. The sergeant said he would take it from there and book the guy. We turned everything over to him and went back into service.

One night, early in my career, we were waiting at the call box to be called in. A motorcycle stopped for the traffic light right beside us. A woman was driving it and she had a male passenger sitting behind her. He looked straight ahead like we wouldn't see him if he didn't look at us. I recognized the way he was acting. He had to be an ex-convict.

I recognized the way he was acting. He had to be an ex-convict.

The light turned green and she started down the street. I told my partner I wanted to check him out. I shifted the car into drive and started after them. I turned on the red lights and told her to pull over with the PA system. She pulled over and my partner started to write down their license plate number as we got out of the cruiser.

Suddenly her passenger grabbed her by the waist and lifted and pushed her forward onto the gas tank. He slid forward on the driver's seat and took control of the motorcycle with her riding on the gas tank in front of him holding onto the handle bars. He was now in control of the motorcycle.

He downshifted the bike and popped the clutch. I knew he was going to run. There was very little traffic on the street now. We climbed back in the cruiser. There was only one cross road and it was several miles down the road. I turned on the siren. We were now in pursuit. I notified radio and gave them our direction of travel. We were going 101 mph.

When my partner was able to get the full license number of the motorcycle, we broke off the pursuit at that time and cut our speed. The road had a sharp dip in it just down the way. When he hit the dip, he dropped down and when he came up out of the dip, he, she, and the bike were airborne and flew through the air for 100 feet. Somehow his front wheel was straight when he landed and he didn't lose it.

This must have scared him because his brake light came on and he was trying to stop. I was pumping my brakes trying to slow down even though I was still two blocks behind him. I didn't know if I would be able to stop in time. I didn't want to hit them.

When he finally got stopped, he got off the bike and put the kick stand down. Then he raised his hands in the air and dropped to his knees. He had done this before.

We cuffed him. The woman was hysterical. She was crying and screaming at him. I asked him why he did such a stupid thing. They could have both been killed or worse yet paralyzed for life.

He said he panicked when we stopped him. He said he was recently released from the state prison and he couldn't take another beating. I said no one was going to beat you. I asked if he had his license reinstated when he was released from the prison. He said he had. He said the woman was his wife and they owned the motorcycle.

I told him we were going to arrest him for willful reckless driving. We asked her if she thought she could get the bike home. It would save them the cost of a tow in and a storage charge. She said she could get the bike home. It was only a few blocks to their house.

I told them he would be able to bond out of jail as soon as he was booked, but the bond would be high. On the way to be booked, he told us he was sorry, but he just panicked. I told him he should be thankful that no one was injured or killed.

He must have pled guilty because we were never subpoenaed to court for his trial. I never had to chase a motorcycle after that.

I was behind a semi-tractor trailer truck once when it made a right-hand turn and in doing so the trailer went up over the curb knocking down a traffic signal on the corner. The light was caught in the under-carriage on the trailer. The light and several feet of electrical wire were pulled out of the ground. This wire became tangled in the rear wheels on the trailer and the light was now being dragged behind the truck.

I managed to get the truck to stop about three blocks down the street. I asked the driver if he knew he struck the traffic light when he made the right-hand turn three blocks back.

He said, "I didn't hit any traffic signal."

I asked him for his driver's license and the registration to the truck. When he gave them to me, I asked him to step out of the truck. I escorted him to the rear of the truck and asked him what that thing was he was dragging behind his truck.

In car accidents, death happens too often.

He said, "I didn't see it."

"I believe you, but I don't know why you didn't hear it with all of the noise it was making."

In car accidents, death happens too often. I investigated a three-car accident during the morning rush hour. The first car had stopped for a red light, the second car stopped behind it, and the third car didn't get stopped in time. It struck car #2 in the rear driving it into the rear of car #1.

A witness stated when car #2 was struck, the driver's head went backward over the back of his seat and when his car hit car #1 his head shot forward striking the steering wheel.

I made the accident report. Two of the cars had to be towed. The face of the driver of car #2 was badly swollen, and I said he should go to the hospital and get checked out.

I transported him to the hospital. He was beaten up but they didn't find any broken bones. He phoned his wife to come and get him. He reassured her he was okay, and she was on the way in. As we waited, we were talking when he straightened up in the chair he was sitting in and fell face first onto the floor.

The doctor was right there. He coded him and they got a cart and wheeled him back into one of the examining rooms closing the door. A short time later a woman came into the ER asking for him. She said she was his wife. The nurse said the doctor was with him now but she would tell him. The woman looked puzzled but she went over and sat down.

The doctor came out of the room and asked for her. The woman identified herself to him. The doctor introduced himself and told her that shortly after her husband called her to pick him up he suffered a massive heart attack. He said they did everything they could to save him but they were not able to. He asked if she would like to see him. She said yes and they went into the room.

I went out to my car and hit in service. I thought to myself what a bummer. An autopsy was performed on the deceased, and the cause of death was indeed a massive heart attack. It had nothing to do with the accident. The man was in his mid-thirties and most often when a person this age has a heart attack it is fatal.

I stopped a car one afternoon. It was being driven in a careless manner. The driver turned out to be a well-known attorney in our city. I asked him for his driver's license and his registration.

He yelled, “Do you know who I am?”

I said, “Yes, I do.”

He gave me his license and registration and I went back to my car to write the ticket. When I went back to his car and gave him the ticket to sign, he said, “I couldn’t have been careless driving; I just pulled out of the parking garage.”

I said, “I know. I almost hit you when you shot out in front of me, and then you accelerated to get through the traffic light when it changed to yellow before you reached the intersection. You were speeding. You made six lane changes without signaling your intent, and you cut three cars off in doing so.”

He signed the ticket and then in a sarcastic voice he said, “I bet your wife must be very proud of you.”

I said, “She is. Isn’t your wife proud of you? Don’t your children run out to greet you when you come home and yell to your wife, ‘Daddy is home, Daddy is home.’”

He didn’t answer. He just drove away.

He pled not guilty in court. I asked the court if I could use my notes to refresh my memory. The judge looked at them and gave them to the defendant and asked if he had any objections to my using them. The defendant looked at them and then checked every page in the book before he said he had no objections.

I presented my evidence using my notes. I never said anything about the defendant’s behavior in court. I didn’t have to. The judge already read it in my notes. The judge found him guilty and told him he got off easy. He said I should have charged him with reckless driving. I thought he would appeal to a higher court but he didn’t.

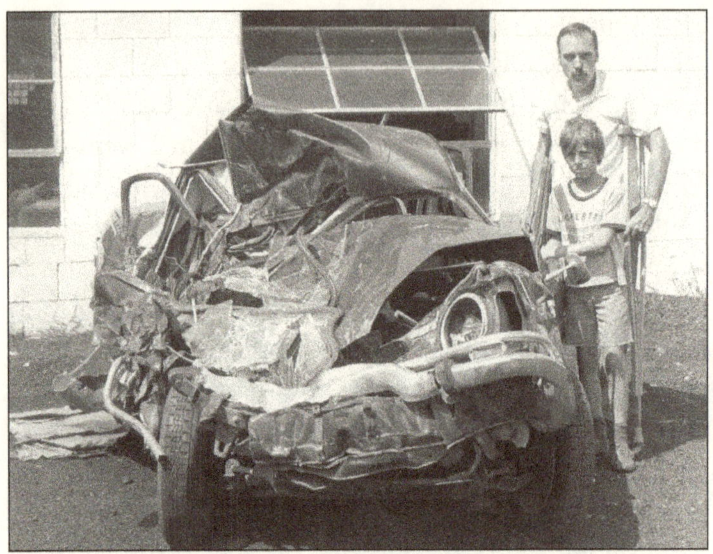

My son and I looked at the wreckage of the car I was driving when I was hit by a drunk driver. If you can't recognize it, the car was a Renault.

My career in traffic was cut short when I was hit head-on by a drunk driver in March 1973. I was off work for eleven months with injuries.

When I came back to work after my accident in February 1974, I was assigned to the jail. I didn't like working there, but it was a job I could do and I was thankful to have it. I kept a low profile. I did my job and never complained. Most of the complaints made against the jail personnel took place when the people were being booked into the jail. I noticed there were no cameras in this area.

I sent an inter-office report to my deputy chief through the chain of command suggesting a video camera be installed in this room with a monitor located where the people being booked could see themselves. They might not be so aggressive if they knew a record of their behavior was being made. The controls and a second monitor could be installed in the uniformed captain's office where he would supervise the operation and maintenance of this equipment. The jail personnel would not be involved in any way with the operation of this equipment.

The equipment was installed and the complaints were all but eliminated.

The food they fed the prisoners was not good, but we were paying a premium price for it. I suggested they buy a hamburger at a drive-in for their evening meal and sweet rolls at the day-old store for their breakfast. Most of the prisoners were only there overnight. This change was a big improvement over what they had been served, and it was less money. The city no longer has a jail, and everything is contracted out to the county corrections facility.

- Twelve -

SOME THINGS ARE MORE DEVASTATING THAN TORNADOES

I was able to transfer out of the jail assignment after a year and go back to the cruiser patrol section.

My first call was to meet with one of my officers who was on a "make an investigation" call. When I arrived on the call, he was waiting on the front porch for me. A woman, he said, was with her daughter who was holding her dead baby. The daughter was refusing to give the body to anyone.

The baby had been dead for several days and had started to decompose.

He said the baby had been dead for several days and had started to decompose. He had notified the county coroner who was sending someone to pick up the baby's body, and the baby's mother would need to go to the hospital for a mental evaluation.

"We'll take her in your car because I don't need the smell in mine," I said. "It will be bad enough just having it in our clothing. We're going to have our hands full when we try to take the baby away from her. We'll have to get her hands cuffed in a hurry, but tell her mother what we are going to do so she will know. You take one arm and I'll take the other and the man from the coroner's office can take the baby."

That's what we did. Once we had her cuffed, she broke down and started to cry. We were able to get her to the hospital without any problems. When we got back to my car, I started the engine and thought to myself maybe I should have stayed in the jail.

Weather in the Midwest is as unpredictable as human behavior. It was 5:00 p.m. one day. I was directing rush hour traffic. It had been raining hard but now it was letting up. I looked to the west and saw a wall cloud about four blocks away from where I was standing. I would estimate it to have been around a thousand feet above the ground. I thought that's the cloud tornadoes come out of. I had seen one many times in a film shown to the police recruits.

I couldn't believe what happened next: a tornado dropped down out of the cloud. It was dark and between 60 and 100 feet long, and the end of it was sweeping in a back-and-forth motion. I stopped the traffic and pointed at the tornado and ran for cover in a multi-story parking garage. I told the people in the garage I just saw a tornado in the air to the west of us.

I looked out in time to see it go back up as it passed over us. I let the cars leave the garage. The tornado touched down in Council Bluffs, Iowa, about three miles east of us causing a lot of property damage, but no lives were lost. They saw it in time to sound a warning.

I will always remember March and May of 1975. One of the worst spring blizzards of our lifetime occurred in March. I was working in the jail on the "C" shift, 4:00 p.m. to midnight. When I left home at 3:00 p.m. to go to work, it was snowing hard and the streets were drifting shut. I should have stayed home then but in those days you went to work even if you had to walk to get there.

I got stuck once at Forty-second and Center but a Good Samaritan gave me a push and I made it on to work. When 5:00 p.m. came, the restaurant that had the contract to feed the people in jail didn't show up. We called them and they said they couldn't get out of their parking lot so they would not be delivering any food tonight.

We phoned several restaurants close by and no one answered. They must have closed due the storm. We had several people in jail that night. We called our supervisor to advise him of the problem and he said he would call us back. He called back in twenty minutes and said to have everyone with minor violations sign their own bonds and let them go if they wanted to leave. Most of them left.

We fed the ones who stayed leftover sweet rolls and coffee, and we shared our lunch with them. When our shift ended most of our relief made it in, but there was no way we could go anywhere so we grabbed a clean blanket and pillow and tried to sleep in one of the empty jail cells. That was the first and hopefully the last night I will ever spend in jail.

> A devastating tornado hit Omaha in May 1975

I didn't get much sleep that night. We were able to dig our way out of the parking lot in the morning. Those of us who had to work that day were rested up when we came back in the afternoon for our shift. I'm glad it was a slow night so everything worked out well for us.

Just a few months later, a devastating tornado hit Omaha in May 1975 and stayed on the ground for a long time, cutting a path through the city two blocks wide and eight miles long.

It was amazing that only three people lost their lives. We were put on twelve-hour shifts with no days off, but that only lasted for fourteen days before we were able to return to our regular shifts.

The city did a remarkable job of cleaning up the rubble after the property owners recovered what they could. It was well organized as bulldozers started on one end of the block and cleared it all the way to the next corner. Then they would go to the next block and start over. Everything was loaded into trucks and hauled to centrally located fields where it was dumped into rows and burned.

This clean-up continued 24/7 for a month. As the fires burned down the rows, the ashes left behind were loaded into trucks and hauled to the land fill. When the fire reached the end of one row, a new row was set on fire. It never stopped.

We were having an addition built on our home when the tornado hit. We were very lucky to have most of it done because the price of building materials skyrocketed due to the shortage of everything caused by the tornado.

I had my first and last helicopter ride during the clean-up operation for the 1975 tornado. It was a military aircraft with no seats and the side doors were removed. I sat on the metal floor wearing a harness that was attached to an eye bolt sticking up out of the floor. This was the only thing that kept me from falling out.

The vibration was really bad as the craft tipped from side to side. I bounced across the floor on my rear. The harness stopped me (and others) just before I might have fallen out, but I sure had a good view of how high up in the air we were.

When we landed I told the captain to find someone else to ride in the helicopter because that was my last ride. He didn't have any trouble finding anyone, but it wasn't my cup of tea. I preferred working with my feet on the ground.

We had a flood on the west end of town. It was 7:00 a.m. when I was dropped off at a bridge to keep everyone off of it. The water was running just below the deck on the bridge. This was before we had portable radios. The whole area had been evacuated, and there was no way for me to contact anyone. I was on my own.

I was told they didn't know what might happen if someone drove on the bridge before it was inspected. Trees, dead cattle, refrigerators, and 55-gallon drums were crashing into the bridge or were jammed up against it. South and east of the bridge was under water for miles and north of the road I was on had been vacated. No one came down the road. I was the only living soul in the area for miles. I borrowed a lawn chair and sat there and watched the different items stack up against the bridge.

Some 55-gallon drums floated down from somewhere. They were pushed up onto the bridge decking. I thought they must be empty to do that. Noon came and went and no one relieved me for lunch. At 2:00 p.m. the water level under the bridge was starting to drop. At 4:00 p.m. no one came to relieve me at shift change. I knew they had forgotten me. What should I do now if I leave and someone goes on the bridge and it collapses? I'm in trouble. I had no way to contact anyone. Some of the junk against the bridge was breaking loose and floating under the bridge.

I ventured out onto the bridge and checked the oil drums on the bridge. They were indeed empty. I rolled them to the end of the bridge and stood them up across the road, blocking the bridge. It was almost 6:00 p.m. I decided I would leave my post and try to find a telephone.

I walked about three blocks when a cruiser came down the road. He stopped and asked, "What are you doing out here?"

I told him I had been out there since before 7:00 a.m. guarding the bridge and they forgot me. I had no way to contact anyone.

I hadn't had any lunch, supper, or water all day and there was no excuse for it. He called his sergeant who took me into the captain's office and told him what happened. The captain shook his head and told me to make out an overtime slip for five hours and he would sign it. I did what he said and went home.

The next morning my lieutenant said how sorry he was that he forgot me. I said to forget it, there was no one around so I didn't have to worry about wetting my pants so no harm was done. What else could I say? He was my boss and would be for a number of years. Everything worked out for the best. We became friends and over time I learned a lot from him. He gave me some good advice, which has helped me through the years.

One winter we had a major three alarm fire at one of the larger grain elevators in the city. The temperature was below zero. The elevators are located in an isolated area at the bottom of a valley next to a railhead surrounded by residential neighborhoods. There is only one entrance into the elevators, which set back about a block from the street. This street was only three blocks long and dead ended on the south side of the elevator company's property.

Traffic control for the police was no problem. Fighting the fire and the cold was a problem for the firefighters. They were able to rotate crews and get into their heated bus out of the cold to warm up, and the Salvation Army was there with hot coffee, donuts, and sandwiches. One could count on them being there.

I don't know what time the first alarm came in. I sent two officers to relieve the dayshift officers at 3:00 p.m. The fire was raging out of control then. The midnight people relieved my people at 11:30 p.m. And the flames were still lighting up the area. The day traffic officers relieved them in the morning when the fire was finally under control. At 3:00 p.m. when my people relieved the day shift, the fire was out. Only steam was rising in the air. They continued to put water into the elevator the rest of the night.

The elevators were still very hot, and they wanted to be sure there were no hot spots that might flame up again. They had another problem: the temperature had dropped below zero and most of their equipment including three fire trucks were frozen to the ground under a foot of ice. The runoff water from the fire had formed a large lake, which froze. The area where they parked most of their equipment was now in the lake. Somehow the firefighters managed to get their equipment dug out the next day, but I have no idea how they did it.

I think back to that night and others when we earned every penny.

The following spring the elevators were torn down and never replaced. I often hear people say how the firefighters and police officers are overpaid, but then I think back to that night and others when we earned every penny. I can recall numerous times when I more than earned every penny I received.

I put in a request to the detective bureau to become a regional investigator. It was a new concept they were going to try, and I was selected to be one of them in 1975. We investigated all types of crimes as they happened or didn't happen.

Fake robberies are a good example of what I mean. I worked several cases where the attendant at a gas station working alone would take the money and make a false report of a robbery to cover the shortage.

In one case I became suspicious when the victim overreacted when he picked the suspect out of a picture line-up. The photo he chose was of a man who was presently serving time in prison.

Later that night I received an anonymous phone call from a woman who said the victim of the robbery was bragging to his friends about how he faked a robbery and was going to meet his accomplice in the parking lot of this grocery store at 10:30 p.m. where they were going to split up the money. I didn't know if this information was any good but it had to be checked out.

Another detective and I were sitting in the cruiser in the parking lot when I saw the alleged victim walk out of the store and get into a car that had just come into the parking lot.

"That's him," I told my partner. "I'll get the driver and you take the passenger."

> We jumped out with our guns drawn and caught them red handed.

My partner hit the gas and that old Ford jumped. We turned the spotlights in their rear window when we stopped behind them. We jumped out with our guns drawn and caught them red handed. They were splitting up the money from the gas station robbery. The money pouch on the seat between them had the name of the owner of the gas station written on it.

I handcuffed the alleged victim and took him back to the police car where we had a nice talk and he spilled his guts. My partner talked to the driver and he also confessed. We impounded their car and took them to the station. They both gave written confessions and were booked.

Another time, I received a call to meet a cruiser car with a cutting call. The rescue squad was leaving when I arrived. The officers had the suspect in handcuffs, and they had one of those box-cutter utility knives with the retractable razor sharp blade that can be replaced when it gets dull. The officers told me the suspect and his wife had been drinking at the bar, came home, and went to bed.

He told her he knew she was sleeping with his best friend but that she wouldn't be doing it any more. She saw he had the knife in his hand. He started stabbing and cutting her between the legs. She was able to hit him in his face with a desk phone and get away. She ran to the neighbors for help. They called the police and the rescue squad.

She suffered numerous lacerations to her genital region. I told the officers to take him down to the jail and book him for felonious assault with a weapon and put my name on the arrest report with them and turn their reports over to the detective lieutenant for me.

I drove to the hospital and was able to talk to the victim before she went to surgery. She said the same things the officers told me. I talked to the doctor who was going to be sewing her up. He said her injuries weren't that serious, but they were going to require a lot of time and a lot of stitches to close all of the lacerations she had. Turns out it took 147 stitches to close up all of her lacerations.

- Thirteen -

MORE STREET STORIES—BURGLARS AND OTHER BAD GUYS

We had a rash of residential burglaries in one area of our district between the hours of 8:00 a.m. and 5:00 p.m. when people were at work. We decided to give this area special attention and patrolled it as much as we could.

As we turned a corner, we observed two young men come out of the front door of one house carrying a huge console television. When they saw us, they dropped the set on the sidewalk and ran down the street.

When the TV hit the sidewalk, of course, it imploded shooting glass in every direction. One of the burglars had on a red nylon windbreaker. I jumped out of the car and went after him. My partner went after the other one with the cruiser.

My guy cut through the houses and I saw him take off his windbreaker and toss it into some bushes. He now had on a yellow pullover shirt. He walked between the houses facing the next street. I picked up the windbreaker and put it inside my jacket as I came out from between the houses.

On the next street I saw my partner had my guy stopped and was talking to him. I trotted down to them and asked, "Have you seen a guy in a red windbreaker running down the street?" He said he did and the guy had gotten into a green car that stopped and they drove away.

I took the windbreaker out of my jacket and asked him if it looked like this one. He didn't say anything. I told him I saw him take off the windbreaker and toss it and I watched him walk out between the houses right into my partner.

We handcuffed him and went back to where they had dropped the TV. It was a total loss. We located the house where they took the TV and had it hauled into our property room. The owner could not identify it as his. The county attorney did not file any charges on him and the guy walked.

Not long after that, we received a burglary in progress call when the owner of a house came home and discovered someone had broken his front door. He heard them walking around upstairs so he went to his car and used his mobile phone to call the police He said they were still in the house when we arrived on the call.

> We found two guys hiding in one of the closets upstairs.

We called for backup, and when they got there they covered the outside of the house and my partner and I and the owner of the house searched the house. We found two guys hiding in one of the closets upstairs. Unbelievable, they were our friends who had dropped the TV on the sidewalk. It is a small world. They weren't so lucky this time. They both went to prison.

When I was still on the "C" shift working 4:00 p.m. to midnight, a stereo store opened in our cruiser district, which was in a high-crime area of the city. I wondered how long it would be before it was robbed or burglarized. The store had not been there a month when we were checking to make sure it was secure.

We checked the front first and everything was okay. Then we drove down the alley behind the building to make sure it was secure. We observed a large truck backed up to their loading dock and two men were loading cartons into it from a four-wheeled cart. The rear door to the store was raised up. They hadn't noticed us because we had our lights turned off.

We notified radio of where we were, what we had, and requested backup. We couldn't see if there was a driver sitting in the truck. It was a good thing the driver had room to make his getaway because I'm sure he would have driven right over us if he had to.

The bad guys started throwing stereos at us so we dropped back.

As we were waiting for our backup to get there, suddenly the truck engine roared and here came the truck. We were lucky the driver turned to his right and headed down the alley away from us. We gave pursuit. The bad guys started throwing stereos at us so we dropped back. The truck was stopped after a short chase when it was blocked in. They still had eleven stereos and twenty speakers in the truck. The store owner was called and said he was on his way down, but he never showed up.

We continued to check the store building after that night. A week later the place was empty and the doors were padlocked. We heard the owner was wanted by the feds and the property in the store had been confiscated by them. The property we recovered must have also been confiscated because it was never sold at the police auction with all of the other unclaimed property. We never went to court on the three people we arrested that night in the truck with the stereo equipment they had taken from the store. I don't know what the story was on them. They could have cut a deal with someone.

It was a slow Sunday morning when I received a radio call on a break-in at a private residence. When I arrived on the call, I was met by two preteen boys who said they had the guy inside the house. I knocked on the door and an elderly woman answered.

She said, "In here, officer."

I followed her into the house and found five people: the elderly woman, an elderly man with a bloody nose and blood covering the front of his shirt, and a couple who appeared to be in their early fifties. A younger black man in his twenties with a badly beaten face and head lay on the floor. I asked what happened.

The older woman said she and her husband had come home from church and discovered the back storm door glass was broken out and the back door was standing open. Her husband told her to go next door and tell John and call the police. She went next door and told John. John went to help her husband and John's wife called the police.

John said when he got there, Ray (the old man) had gone into the house so he went after him. He yelled for Ray and Ray answered saying, "I'm in the bedroom."

He said he ran into the bedroom and Ray was sitting on this man's chest hitting him with his fists. Ray had a bloody nose.

John told him to stop. Ray was bleeding all over the guy and the man's face was badly beaten. Ray told John he had heard someone in the house so he went in and found the guy in their bedroom. He was filling up one of their pillow cases from their bed with his wife's jewelry. He yelled at the man to stop and the guy punched him in the face giving him a bloody nose.

Ray said, "Is that all you've got?" and hit the man with a left upper cut right on the chin and then followed through with a right cross smashing his face and the man went down. Ray said he was about out of gas, so he fell on the guy and was hitting him when John came into the room. Ray had been on the Army boxing team in WWII, but that was a long time ago.

I asked him how old he was: seventy-nine. He said after he hit the guy he didn't dare stop or the guy might have killed him, so he just kept pounding away for as long as he could. He was sure glad when John got there when he did because he was ready to quit.

> He said after he hit the guy he didn't dare stop or the guy might have killed him.

I think it was a good thing the bad guy was knocked out with the second punch. I asked Ray if he wanted to go to the hospital for a check-up and he said he was okay. I called the rescue squad for the burglar and had a police hold put on him at the hospital. I called the detective bureau and told them what I had. They said they would send the crime lab out for possible prints and pictures and to bring my reports to them.

I talked to Ray and told him the next time this happens wait for the police to come. I said, "He might have had a gun."

One of Ray's sons bought the house next to mine. He said Ray was still in good health then. Ray lived well into his nineties. His family still talks about the time he came home from church and caught the burglar in their house. He was a tough old geezer.

We reported on duty at 7:30 one morning and received a call to see a party about a noise complaint. The address was to a two-story home that had been converted into four apartments: two upstairs and two on the main floor. The party who called was a woman who lived on the first floor.

We could hear what sounded like a vacuum cleaner running in the apartment across the hall from her. She said it had been running all night. She hated to call because the old man who lived there was such a nice person, but she had been up all night.

We knocked on his door but no one answered. We went outside and tried to look in through the windows. My partner called, “Come look at this.”

Through the window we could see the old man slumped over sitting in a rocking chair. His mouth had duct tape over it, and his arms and one leg were taped to the chair. His other leg was free, and a canister-type vacuum cleaner was running beside him.

Through the window we could see the old man slumped over sitting in a rocking chair. His mouth had duct tape over it.

We hurried into the house and asked the woman if anyone had a key to his apartment, but she didn't know. We were going to kick the door in when my partner discovered it was open. Someone had already kicked it in.

We removed the tape from the old man's mouth. He could hardly talk. He needed some water. I got him a glass while my partner freed him from the chair. He said someone had knocked on his door the night before at 8:30 p.m. He was going to put the chain on the door before he opened it, but they crashed right through the door pulling the chain out of the wall.

He said they had a gun and robbed him before they gagged him and taped him to the chair. They searched through the whole apartment before they left. He tried to get loose but wasn't able to. The tape was too strong. He was finally able to free his right leg, so he turned on the vacuum cleaner with his foot. It was still plugged in from when he had used it a day earlier. He thought someone would hear it running and call the police. He was not able to move the chair. He said the men were black, but he couldn't identify them because they both had something covering their faces.

When no one came, he thought he was going to die there. When we finally came in, he knew he was going to be all right. He refused to go to the hospital.

We called the crime lab and the detective bureau. The crime lab did get some prints; the detective bureau said to make the report and bring it in. We contacted the man's children and stayed with him until they got there. The woman who called in the noise complaint felt bad because she didn't call in sooner. We never heard any more about the case.

We had a shoplifter call at one of our Mom and Pop grocery stores one afternoon. They were holding a man who put a sack of candy in his overcoat pocket. When he checked out, he never paid for it. We made the reports and took the bag of candy as evidence.

He had two chickens in each leg.

As we were putting the suspect in the cruiser, I noticed his legs didn't look right. He had baggy pants on. I told him to get out of the car and I patted his lower legs down. He had something in his pants. We took him back into the store and had him drop his pants. He had a pair of booster pants on under his baggy ones. He had two chickens in each leg. This guy was a professional booster (shoplifter).

I had never seen booster pants before, so we held them as evidence. Booster pants have an elastic waist band so they can be pulled open quickly and something can be dropped into them. They snap closed even faster. The pants only reach to the knees, and they have drawstrings on the cuffs so they can be tightened and nothing will fall out the bottom of them. They are worn under baggy pants that hide the stolen merchandise. Some are lined with foil so the wearer can walk through a scanner without being detected. There are booster bags, coats, and other devices. Professional shoplifters or organized shoplifter groups are called boosters.

Out of the hundreds of shoplifters I arrested, only three of them were kleptomaniacs. In other words, people who have an irresistible urge to steal even small cheap items. All were from well-to-do families.

One was a woman who had to take one tube of lipstick every time she went into a store, and her family owned a chain of stores that sold lipstick. The second was a male interior designer who owned his own company. He had to steal a package of cheap plastic ballpoint pens if he saw them when he went into a store, and the third was also well known and wealthy. He shopped at the same grocery store every week for years, and each week he took a package of shoelaces.

The store's new manager was told about this practice. He said he wasn't going to put up with him doing it anymore and had the man arrested twice. I think he must have taken his shoplifting to some other store in a different district because we never saw him after that.

Before the advent of the clothes dryer, people use to dry their laundry by hanging it outside on a device called a clothesline. Every household had one and it was usually located in the backyard. I have taken numerous reports on items stolen from clotheslines when the owners forgot to take them in before it got dark. Any item left on the clothesline was fair game for a thief.

One night I took a report of a stolen corset from a clothesline. The owner was a large woman. She said she washed it at night and hung it out to dry after dark because she was embarrassed and didn't want her neighbors to see how large it was. She said she could not go to work until she bought another one. She said they were quite expensive. I didn't even want to think about what type of person would have taken it.

I met a retired officer at a luncheon recently whom I had not seen in twenty years. It was sort of odd because I had just told someone about an incident he and I were involved in. It happened in June 1974. An auto dealership had requested special attention for their business because they were having problems with thieves breaking into cars on their lot and stealing the stereo equipment and other items they wanted.

The dealer was in the process of having the lot made more secure and having new lighting installed. Until the construction was completed, they wanted the police to check their lot more often at night. I was driving by their lot at 9:30 one night and noticed a man in one of their cars. He ducked down when he saw the cruiser.

I drove right on past him and stopped down the street where I knew he could not see me. I called radio and told them where I was and what I had and asked for a backup. I was north of the lot and wanted my backup to stop south of the lot where they could not be seen. We would walk into the lot, and the thieves probably would not see us. I gave them a description of the car they were in.

I stuck my shotgun against the window and said, "I want you to get out of the car real slow and place your hands on top of the car."

I saw the cruiser coming. He turned off his lights. He pulled over and stopped out of their view. I told him over the radio that I saw him and I was going to be walking next to the buildings coming his way. I saw him get out of his car.

He said, "I see you now."

We walked right up on the car. Two men inside it never saw us coming. We turned our mag lights on their faces and yelled, "Police. Put your hands on the dashboard where we can see them." They did as they were told.

The man sitting behind the steering wheel said, "We're FBI."

I stuck my shotgun against the window and said, "I want you to get out of the car real slow and place your hands on top of the car and then step back and spread your legs."

He said again, "We're FBI."

I said, "Do it now," and I motioned with my shotgun.

He got out slowly and assumed the position. He said his ID was in the right side pocket of his jacket. They were indeed FBI. They had a tip that an escaped convict from Indiana was going to be at the house across the street from the car lot, and we blew it for them.

I told them they were the ones who blew it. They should have notified us they were going to be there.

I said, "We did our job right. Maybe you should do yours the same way."

He shut up and we left.

The car dealer called our deputy chief the next day and wanted to thank us for checking his lot. The chief said we handled the situation very well. Apparently the FBI had already filled him in.

I thought to myself the chief must not have been talking to the agent who was in the lot the night before.

I will never forget this one hot afternoon in August 1968. A cruiser was in pursuit of a vehicle used in a robbery. The stick-up man crashed the getaway car while trying to turn a corner. He fled on foot running into an overgrown weed field that lay between the road and some railroad tracks. The field covered an area one block wide by eight blocks long. It was full of sunflowers, tumbleweeds, stick tights, thistles, sandburs, and mosquitoes. There was no breeze at all.

Officers were called in to search the field. The first officers to arrive were assigned to watch the perimeter of the field in case the party ran out.

The rest of us lucky ones lined up with our shotguns at ready and moved into the field. The sunflowers were over our heads and they were so thick you could hardly walk through them. The tumbleweeds came up to our knees and grabbed at our legs. The thistles, sandburs, and stick tights covered our trousers and they were in our socks. The sweat was pouring out of us and the mosquitoes were having a field day. The weeds were covered with dust and when we brushed against one the dust fell on us. The sunflower leaves scratched our faces and arms and when the sweat and dust got into the scratches, it really burned. We could hardly breathe it was so hot and there was no air movement.

We should have known if the suspect was still in the field the mosquitoes would have sucked all of his blood out by then. When we finally reached the end of the field, the officers stationed there said no one came out of the field except us. I don't think we missed anybody in there, but we could have. I think he must have slipped away before we got organized. We were really a mess when we came out of that field, and to add insult to injury the bad guy got away.

In the thirty years I was on the job I only had one bad guy that I know of who cased my home. I don't know who his intended target was going to be: my family or me. This guy was a known burglar and he was no good. The courts have ruled that burglars are considered to be nonviolent criminals so I might not have had any reason to react the way I did.

I went to a preliminary hearing for him one morning at 9, and he was bound over to the district court to stand trial for burglary. When he was led away by the court officer, he gave me a dirty look and whispered something at me, which I didn't understand.

I had another trial after that and then I had lunch with a friend of mine. I got home around 1:00 p.m. and my next door neighbor was standing on his front door stoop. I walked over to talk to him. We lived on a dead-end street, and our addresses were wrong. We lived in the 7400 block but our house numbers were 7100.

> "If something happens to me, there will be 400 blue shirts looking for you."

We saw a car coming up the hill toward us going very slowly and I recognized the driver. It was the burglar that I had appeared against in court that morning. He lived twenty miles away on the other side of town. What was he doing here driving up my dead-end street?

I couldn't take a chance when he stopped his car to turn around in the street. I ran out to him. He was surprised I drew my off-duty revolver and pointed it at his head.

I told him, "You SOB, you know where I live now, so I'm only going to tell you one time. If something happens to my family, I'm coming after you; and if something happens to me, there will be 400 blue shirts looking for you."

My neighbor called the police and they towed the burglar's car and arrested the bad guy. I never heard any more about it. He must have cut a deal because he pled guilty to burglary and got a lot of time for it. I never saw him after that or ever heard his name again.

My family never knew about this incident and there was no need to tell them. He may have inadvertently turned into my street, but my gut feeling says no way. He was up to no good and I made the right decision.

A grave stone was discovered on the front porch of a house where a popular fourteen-year-old girl lived after someone had rung the door bell and ran. The cruiser officer thought it may have come from a small cemetery that was nearby. I wrote down the information they had and told them to call in for an RB number (RB stands for Record Bureau; every piece of evidence has a number) so I could have it for my follow-up report. They called for a truck to pick up the stone and take it to the property room. I couldn't do much with it since everything was closed.

I discovered there were eighteen cemeteries in the city and eight of them were on the side of town where the stone was left on the front porch. The next morning I phoned all but three of the cemeteries and the stone didn't come from any of them.

That afternoon when I went to work I went to one of the cemeteries and found out the stone didn't come from there, but they had the phone number of the caretaker of one of the two I had left to contact. I phoned him and no luck so far. I was batting zero.

I had one cemetery left to check. It had to have come from there if it had been taken from one of our local cemeteries. No such luck. I struck out. I made out my report, put the RB number on it, and turned it in. I couldn't do anymore. Perhaps one of the kids who put the stone on the porch will tell someone someday and the mystery will be solved.

When I was a regional investigator, one of the district cruiser officers called and asked me to meet him with a residential burglary. Someone had broken in a house through the front door and stolen an antique cherry-wood curved-glass-front china cabinet while the home owners were at work. The officer said this was the second day-time residential burglary he had in the last six weeks, and antique furniture was taken in both of them.

I looked over the officer's report and noticed the value of the cabinet was listed as $2,000. The owner had recently inherited it from her mother and had to have it appraised for insurance coverage. It had been in her family since the 1860s. She had the original bill of sale for it and it had a number on it that matched one on a tag on the back of the cabinet. She had used a dealer in town to appraise it for the insurance company.

I went down to police headquarters and looked up the other burglary: an antique desk was stolen in that one. I phoned the people and told them who I was. I asked her if she had had her desk appraised for the insurance company. Yes, she had. She used the same dealer the other party had and I asked her a couple more questions about something on her report. I told her that was all I needed and thanked her before I hung up.

I completed my follow-up report on the second burglary and made out an information report on the first one. I took them to my lieutenant. He got a big grin on his face. The next morning two detectives made a visit to the antique dealer and recovered the china cabinet. The antique dealer wasn't a happy camper when he was arrested.

The news media picked up on this and had a field day with it. The dealer finally pled guilty to possession of stolen property and went out of business shortly after that. Thanks to an alert officer on the street, two cases were closed and there was one happy woman when she got her antique china cabinet back.

Thanks to an alert officer on the street, two cases were closed.

While I was in the Air Force serving overseas, I was not aware that our police department had had a burglary scandal. I understand several officers had been terminated and some command officers including the chief were demoted. Prior to being assigned to the midnight shift after I graduated from recruit training, I still had not heard much about it.

I had been working on the street less than a month when we received a call of a residential burglary. The woman who called stated she was on her way home from work, and when she turned into her driveway, she saw two men come out of her front door. They saw her and both of them ran down the street. She went next door to her neighbor's and woke them up. She called the police from their house.

When we arrived on the call, we checked the house and no one was in it. But the burglars had placed about a dozen 16 mm movie projectors and screens by the front door where they could move them out of the house in a hurry.

The woman told us her husband was a police detective. My partner was making the report when her husband came home. He looked around and said, "I'm Sergeant Dipshitsky. Give me your report. I'll take care of it and you can go back in service."

When we got back in the cruiser I asked my partner why someone would have so many movie projectors. He said he didn't know. Then he said, "You're on probation, so don't say anything about this call to anyone unless you are asked."

I noticed he didn't hit back in service, but I didn't say anything. He drove down to the police station and parked in front of the station instead of parking inside the garage like we normally would have.

He said to wait in the cruiser. He was gone for about twenty minutes.

When he came back, he hit in service and we drove back to our district. He never said what he was doing in the station and I never asked. I didn't want to know. I was still on probation.

> Sometimes the bad guys were our guys.

I read in the local newspaper that a detective sergeant had been relieved of duty following a long investigation of a break-in at a warehouse. Ten 16 mm movie projectors and other items were recovered from the home of Sergeant Robert Dipshitsky. I now knew why he had so many projectors. The sergeant was terminated following a ten-day suspension.

Another detective, Sergeant Stu Pidity, was under investigation. A typewriter taken in a burglary he investigated turned up in a repair shop and it was traced back to him. He was later terminated. Sometimes the bad guys were our guys.

Harold's Market was a grocery store in East Omaha located on East Locust Street. Harold Oberman was the owner of the store. I remember when he bought a new safe he said, "I would like to see them get in this one." He put it against the east wall of the store where it was visible from the street. The police cruisers could check it when they drove by, and he left the lights on in the store all night.

The store building was made out of cement blocks. One night around 3:00 a.m. the store's alarm was set off by someone breaking in the front door. When the cruiser got there, the safe was gone and there was a huge hole in the east wall where the safe had been. Dual tire tracks were pressed into the sod going up to the outside of the building where the safe had been.

There had to be two people involved in this caper because one person could not have done it in such a short timeframe. They punched two holes through the cement blocks, one on each side of where the safe was. One person broke through the front door setting off the alarm and ran over to the safe getting the tow cable from the person on the outside of the store through the hole in the wall. They had wrapped the tow cable around the safe and handed it back to the person on the outside through the hole in the wall on the other side of the safe. This person had hooked the cable together and winched the safe outside of the store through the block wall onto the tow truck and drove away.

The next morning one of the car dealers downtown reported their tow truck had been stolen during the night. That afternoon someone reported a tow truck and a safe on the river side of the levee south of Eppley Airfield. The robbers had been successful in getting into the safe. I don't believe they were ever apprehended. We didn't always get the bad guys.

- Fourteen -

BOMBS AND BULLETS JUST LIKE ON TV

I now had enough seniority to hold the day shift, and I heard they needed a sergeant in the training section. Since I had a college degree, I qualified for the position. Not only was it a day job, but the position holder also had the weekends off. I had never had a job with the weekends off since before I was on the police department.

I applied for the opening in 1976 and was accepted. I attended the Traffic Institute at Northwestern University in Evanston, Ill., to become a police instructor and received my certificate to teach from the Nebraska Law Enforcement Training Center. I was assigned to the training section from 1976 to 1984. I was the Training Commander when I transferred out.

I never realized the amount of work you must do in preparing for a police recruit class. Ordering all of the supplies you will need for the class: pencils, pens, paper, notebooks, textbooks. Updating lesson plans.

Scheduling outside instructors can sometimes be a challenge especially if they were only going to be available at the same time. Fortunately this did not happen often, but when it did we had people on our staff who taught the subject.

Our curriculum far exceeded the requirements set by the state to become a certified police officer. We had an outstanding training staff when I was there. All of our instructors were committed to what they were teaching.

We brought our accident investigators into the twentieth century with our accident reconstruction classes.

We updated the shotguns issued to officers. Our shotguns needed replacing as they were old and worn out. Even worse, they were designed for hunting upland game but not for police service. The problems: a sawed-off barrel with the bead sight improperly placed back on the end of the barrel. A cut-off choke, which shortened the effective range of the weapon. These poor modifications rendered the weapon almost useless.

At 200 feet if aimed at the center of a man's back, the shot would be above the man's head and it would have spread enough to miss him. The finish on the gun would not hold up bouncing around in the rack in a cruiser, and we needed a gun that will hold more than three rounds.

So we designed a police shotgun and met with a Remington Arms representative to see if they would manufacture them for us and what the cost would be. The rep was interested and said he would have to check with the office. He said they made one close to the one we wanted for the Secret Service, but they were not allowed to make them for anyone else.

He called about a week later and said he wanted to make us an offer. They would make us the number of shotguns we wanted for a lower price than we expected. In return they wanted the right to manufacture and sell this gun to other law enforcement agencies. We told him we would have to run this offer past our chief.

Less than a month later we had the 125 guns we ordered. They were far superior to the scatter guns we were using. The new shotguns hit where they were aimed, and the choke held the shot in a tighter pattern for a longer distance. The magazine held four more rounds, and the finish we chose for the weapon was holding up well. We were satisfied with the shotgun.

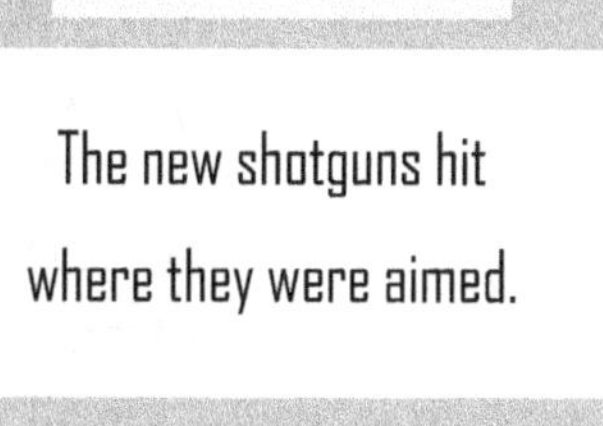

We ran tests on the different buck shot and found the #2 buck shot was best suited for our work in an urban area. We submitted our findings to the chief's office, and we received our letter back telling us to stay with the ammunition we were presently using.

All of our officers received training with the new shotgun before it went into service. We made a training film showing them the proper way to load and unload the weapon and how to operate it. Then we practiced by shooting some blue rock (clay pigeons tossed in the air).

I showed each of them a picture of where they should be aiming when the rock is going away from them. I told them when the target reaches its zenith and starts to drop, it would look like it stopped moving and to pull the trigger then. I instructed each one of them as they shot, and they started to hit them.

With the old scatter gun some of the people had never hit one before. Some were now shooting ten in a row and they were enjoying it. Some of the officers thanked me for taking the time to help them. They said no one had ever done that before.

Recently, my wife and I were watching a police show on TV. A uniformed officer with a shotgun was running for cover. I said, "Would you look at that! He has the shotgun I helped to design. It is a small world isn't it."

In addition to training the police recruits, we had in-service training for all of our sworn personnel plus the regular qualification shoots. We trained the Emergency Reaction Unit (aka SWAT) people and assisted the sniper team with their practice shoots. Offutt Air Force Base asked for a copy of the ERU section in our standard operation procedures manual, and parts of it were used as a model when they wrote their manual.

I discovered you don't have to be a good police officer to be a good SWAT member or a sniper. They are completely different jobs. One outstanding member of the team was a mediocre police officer. One of his command officers was determined to have him removed from the team as punishment for an infraction he was charged with. I was able to show removing him from the team would not improve his performance as a police officer but might hurt the performance of the SWAT. He held a critical position on the team and his removal could have had an adverse effect on his team members. We didn't need the problems it could create.

The command officer pushing for his removal was one of the stinkers. He was later found to be involved in something he should not have been and was terminated. Few tears were shed when that happened, and I know there were some smiling faces around when the announcement was released.

The Nebraska Eastern Gun Club allowed our police sniper team to practice on their range. The training staff worked in the pits, and the Training Commander stayed with the shooters. They used .243 caliber rifles sighted in at different ranges. They were all expert marksmen. Working the pit was quite an experience and one I'll never forget.

> We located what we thought was a bomb on a window ledge.

We had a very professional SWAT team for our days. I understand today's team is second to none and that is the way it should be.

The training staff attended several classes at the air base, and we found them to be beneficial. We also taught recruits from other police departments, railroad special agents, and firefighters who needed state certification as police officers before they could become arson investigators.

Prior to the booby trap bomb that took the life of one of our officers in 1970 and before we had a bomb squad, my partner and I received a radio call of a possible bomb in a window well at one of the downtown banks.

We located what we thought was a bomb on a window ledge on the south side of the building next to the alley. Someone had used black electrical tape to hold it together. It contained three sticks of dynamite, a blasting cap, a battery, and a wind-up alarm clock. They had removed the glass covering from the face of the clock and attached a wire from the battery to the minute-hand on the clock. A screw went through the face of the clock so the minute-hand would make contact with it when it came around. One wire from the blasting cap was attached to the screw. The other wire from the cap went to the battery.

It should have blown up but it hadn't. My partner and I had both been in the service so we knew not to touch it. We blocked the alley with our car and moved the people out of the surrounding buildings.

We phoned the detective bureau and told them what we had, and they sent out a man who had been trained by the military to disarm bombs. He looked at it and said it was a live one.

He needed a pair of dikes to disarm it. A maintenance man from the bank gave him a pair. He told us to stop everyone from walking across the alley in case it ignited. He walked into the alley. A few minutes later he walked out of the alley carrying the device in his hands. He had cut the wires. He said he had to check it real good before he cut anything. The only reason it did not explode was because the paint on the clock hands was thick enough to stop the electrical current from making a complete circuit.

If the person who made the device had checked the electrical circuit prior to attaching the dynamite cap, he would have known it wouldn't work and this story would have had a different ending.

I can only imagine the rush the bomber must have felt when he placed the bomb on the window ledge knowing the carnage it was intended to cause. Think of the disappointment he must have felt when it didn't happen, yet he dared not go back to see why for fear of being caught.

Our bomb expert said to bring the original report into the detective bureau when we finished it. We had no idea how long the device had been there. When we took the report into the bureau, everyone was talking about the bomb. They all agreed we were lucky it turned out the way it did. Whoever made the bomb and put it there was never apprehended.

I was sure glad when they organized the bomb squad because we needed one. I had four bomb calls prior to when they organized the bomb squad, including the bomb in the bank window. I cleared the area and waited for the experts to come and take care of them.

The experts had to come from Fort Leonard Wood in Missouri for one of them since it was a military device. It made for a long day just sitting there waiting for them to get here. One call was a briefcase sitting by the side of the police headquarters building. The owner of the briefcase, a police officer, had set it down while talking to a friend and forgot it when he left. He came back to get it while we were waiting for our expert to arrive.

Another bomb call turned out to be an anniversary clock sent to a woman from her son in Vietnam. She didn't know what was in the package when it came. She heard a ticking sound in the box but it had stopped. She thought it might be a bomb and she wanted it checked.

Once it was formed, the bomb squad had a lot of neat equipment. The bomb trailer was impressive but it was even more so when they detonated a device in it.

It was a calm day when I first witnessed the bomb trailer being used. The blast was directed up into the air, and the debris shot several hundred feet up followed by a perfect smoke ring. They had a water cannon that was used on briefcases and suitcases to open them up and disable the bomb if there was one. It worked very well.

They used liquid nitrogen to freeze the batteries on the bombs to disable them and deactivate the bomb. I was surprised by the large amount of outdated explosive material that was turned into the bomb squad by different places each year to be disposed of.

After one of the recruit classes graduated, I was having some health problems. I read about a police department having a lead problem with their indoor range, and two of their officers were suffering from lead poisoning. My symptoms were the same as theirs.

I called my private doctor to do a test on my blood for lead. My test results came in and my blood lead level was high. The doctor advised me to stay out of the gun range until it was cleared as being the source where I was getting the lead. I told my supervisor what the doctor had said, and he arranged to have all of the training personnel tested for lead. Three of the seven of us had elevated lead levels.

My supervisor met with the Chief of Police and I was called to his office. He challenged me for thinking my lead problem came from the range. I told him that I never said it did, but it could have. I told him I thought the range should be checked and if there is a problem it should be corrected.

The range was found to have a major problem with the ventilation system. The range was shut down while a new ventilation system was installed, and the whole range was renovated.

We did a lot of testing of police equipment in the training section. One time a uniformed captain brought a shield used in riot control into the training office and wanted to see if it was bulletproof.

We went down to the gun range, and he told the range officer he would hold the shield while he shot it. The range officer looked at me and I told the captain, "Range rules prevent us from firing a weapon when someone is down range. We will have to set your shield in front of the bullet stops at the back end of the range."

The range officer fired six rounds at the shield. When he brought the shield back to us, it had six holes in it. I told the captain I didn't think it was made to stop bullets. The captain looked at it and agreed. I think he realized that holding the shield while someone shot at it was not a good idea after all.

We also tested a bulletproof clipboard that failed the test. I know they must have sold thousands of them to the different police departments across the country. It was a nice looking clipboard but don't try to stop a bullet with it. We also tested a zinc bullet made for indoor ranges.

It eliminated the lead gases that were created by a lead bullet when it passes through a gun barrel. It did stop the lead gases since there was no lead in them. They were hard on the bullet stops and over time it could be a problem. Costwise the lead was cheaper because the lead bullets were salvaged and sold to a foundry.

The police cruiser was a regular standard four-door passenger car.

When I started with the police department in the late 1950s, most of our equipment was not originally manufactured for police use. The rotating red light, for example, was manufactured for use on aircraft. The shotgun was made for the sportsman. They sawed off the barrel and put the bead sight back on the barrel for looks and called it a police riot gun.

The police cruiser was a regular standard four-door passenger car made for civilian use as were the spotlights. It is unknown where the sirens came from. They were too bulky and heavy to be attached to the cars built after the 1950s. The metal on the cars was not strong enough to hold them. We did not have sirens on our cars for several years.

Eventually, a siren was bolted on the left front fender, and the siren switch was located on the floor just to the left of the steering column. All the driver had to do to operate the siren was press the switch down with his left foot.

There were a couple of problems with this type of siren. It took so much electrical current to operate it, even with the new 12-volt systems on the cars and the alternating current generators, if the driver held the switch down for very long, the car's engine would cut out and stall.

Also, with the lighter gauge sheet metal being used on the construction of the cars, heavy sirens were pulling out of the fenders. The rotating red light on the roof and the police radio in the trunk also used a lot of electricity. The larger amp alternator helped to correct this problem, but it was the new technology in the electronics that finally eliminated these problems and made it possible for computers to be used in the patrol cars.

When I joined the police department, there were several older men working in the cruisers who weighed over 300 pounds. They broke down the seats in every car they drove. The garage tried to repair them by bolting two-by-fours to the underside of the seat frame beneath what was left of the springs to hold them up. They filled the hole on the top of the seat with material from old Army blankets. It worked for a while, but never long enough.

Some of the younger officers with the smaller rear ends carried a piece of plywood to put on the seat to cover the hole so we wouldn't fall into it when we were assigned to use one of these cars.

The car seats are made so much better today so they don't break down like they used to. There doesn't seem to be as many heavy people on the job like there were but that can change.

In the 1960s some companies began manufacturing equipment for police use. Some of the first items were the overhead light bar, the electronic siren, and the transistor radio. Our radio was attached under the dashboard; the control box for the siren, PA system, and overhead lights was mounted on the top of the dashboard. The shotgun and a fire extinguisher and shotgun holder were mounted on the dashboard and on the floor.

One of my partners wondered why they didn't make a rack and stack everything on it together where it would be out of the way and easy for the driver to operate. I suggested he design one.

He made a rough drawing on the back of one of our report forms. The next thing he did was stop at one of the garages in our district where he knew the owner. He and the owner came out of the shop to the cruiser. The owner had a tape measure. He measured everything and said, "No sweat, I'll have it for you tomorrow."

The next day we took our lunch break there and they installed a rack in less than ten minutes. It looked good, very professional and everything fit perfectly. My partner asked him what we owed him and he said a couple of beers would be fine. My partner dropped off a six pack on his way to work the next day.

When we picked up our car at detail change, the garage foreman wanted to see us. He wanted to know where we got that rack. My partner said he made it. The foreman asked what it cost him to make it. He said a couple of bucks. The foreman said, "I'm going to reimburse you out of petty cash. We want to put them in all of the cruisers."

I grinned at my partner. He made fifty cents on the deal and we had a nice piece of equipment that held all of our electric equipment together where they could be operated by the driver of the cruiser.

The automobile industry finally started to manufacture a vehicle made for commercial use. They called it a police package. The cruisers contained heavy-duty parts where regular parts were wearing out first: transmission, suspension, steering, door hinges, front seats, and seat cover material. It was prewired for the roof lights, and the spotlights came as part of the package that also included a heavy-duty alternator and a certified speedometer. It was a big improvement over what we had been using.

The equipment they are using today is far superior to what we had in my time and that is the way it should be. Electronic sirens replaced the motor-driven ones. Transistors replaced the vacuum tubes in the radio. Strobe lights replaced the motor-driven rotating red lights and LED lights are replacing the incandescent bulbs. All of these items are energy-saving devices. The vehicles are now made to last far longer than they were.

After-market products are available to convert cars into police vehicles. For example, the rear seat and the divider between the rear seat and the trunk is removed. All knobs and handles are removed from the rear doors, and a new heavy vinyl plastic interior is installed in the vehicle. It is molded to fit the interior of the car.

Steel bars cover the windows in the doors and the rear window. The driver of the car is protected by steel bars, steel plates, and lexan (a plastic sheeting).

The rear seat is now part of the plastic interior. It has been molded into the shape of a seat so the whole caged area can be hosed out when it needs to be cleaned. Once a party is placed in the cruiser, he or she is not going anywhere until someone lets them out. The driver can change the color of the overhead lights with a flip of the switch. They can be red, white, blue, yellow, or a combination of all of the colors.

The new flood lights on the overhead bar can light up a street with a blinding light from two blocks away. It is unbelievable until you see it.

Over my thirty-year career, I saw plenty of other changes. When I first went on the job it was known as the police department and then it later became the police division, now it is once again the police department.

The last year the city bought black-and-white police cars was 1956 until they were reintroduced in the 1990s. The light blue necktie was replaced with a black one. The black necktie was worn in the late 1940s before it was replaced with the light blue necktie.

We didn't have a shoulder patch then. Now they have two of them—one on each shoulder. The navy blue uniform has now been replaced with a black one. None of these items has anything to do with the effectiveness of the department. I just found it interesting how things change.

We wore the same wool pants all year long and they were so warm, especially because cruisers didn't have air conditioning at first. We did have a short-sleeved summer shirt called an air flow. The command staff determined the date when we would start wearing them and the date when we had to stop wearing them. Everyone dressed in the same uniform then. We were finally allowed to wear light-weight trousers during the summer months.

We had to wear our hats in the cruiser at all times. We had to look professional in our sweat-soaked uniforms with the sweat dripping off our chins because someone might see us. After dark the hats came off and we would stop at a gas station and run cold water over our wrists to cool off. When we finally got the air conditioned cars, we really appreciated them. Looking back I don't know how we ever got by without them.

When I came on the job, some of the cars still had only one-way radios. Radio would give you a call and repeat it two more times. When you completed the call, you would drive to a police call box and advise radio. At first, police officers still worked as relief radio operators. There was only one radio channel for the whole department then.

When I came on the job, some of the cars still had only one-way radios.

We still had officers on job who had ridden the motorcycles with the side cars on them during the 1930s and 1940s. They worked out of pill boxes located at different locations in the city. I remember the one at Thirtieth and Cuming when I was a child. I have no idea why they called them a pill box. It may have been because they were so small. They had room inside for the motorcycle with its sidecar, a table, two chairs, the telephone, and a wood-burning heating stove. No one ever said anything about a bathroom. They surely had one or we would have heard about it.

Two officers were stationed to a pill box, and they received all of their calls over a telephone. They would make the call and return to the pill box where they would phone the station and let them know the call was completed. If they made an arrest on the call, a paddy wagon was sent out to transport the arrest to the station house. They talked about heating bricks on the stove and putting them into the sidecar to keep their feet warm when they went on a call. This sounded good but I don't know if it really happened.

At a staff meeting when the Gene Leahy Mall was first built downtown, I suggested using bicycles to patrol it. I was almost laughed out of the room. Today you see bicycles hanging from carriers on the backs of the cruisers all over the city.

When the K-9 patrol unit was introduced in the 1960s, it was a big success, and the dogs and their officers apprehended a lot of burglars. One of the first calls I made where a dog was used was a break-in at a laundry. The dog went in first before we entered the building. The dog picked up the burglar's scent where he entered the building and followed it to one of their large washing machines where he started to bark.

We flipped open the lid on the washing machine and there our burglar was.

The dog handler said, "I think he found something."

We flipped open the lid on the washing machine and there our burglar was. The dog handler told him to come out or he would send the dog in after him. The burglar climbed out. I don't think we ever would have looked in the machines for a burglar.

On another call the burglar had left before we arrived. The handler said he was going to turn the dog loose. He turned on a blinking red light that was attached to the dog's vest so we could follow him in the dark. He said if the burglar didn't get in a car, the dog would get him.

The dog didn't go a block when he had something. We heard screaming, yelling, barking, and growling. When we reached him, the man was on the ground rolled up in the fetal position. The dog had him. The man suffered a few bites, and the dog was very excited about catching a bad guy.

The dogs were also very good on crowd control. On a long leash they could sure move a crowd in a hurry. When the dogs got older and they had to be retired, and they never replaced them.

Years later they brought the dogs back, but they are now trained as drug and bomb dogs. There is a need for them.

Our first helicopters were Army surplus. As I recall most of the pilots then received their training at a local college. They flew those Huey helicopters for years. At first the news media reported something on them every night. Every move they made was covered. Once the newness wore off, the news coverage dwindled. Those helicopters were replaced with new ones straight from the factory, and they are equipped for police use. The news media must not find them newsworthy since little is ever said about them now.

They are an excellent piece of equipment for law enforcement. In fact, it is unbelievable what they are capable of doing. It is too bad they are so expensive. In our present economic times it is hard to justify having one. Perhaps it is best to keep them in a low profile out of the news.

- Fifteen -

POLICE RECRUIT TRAINING—CREATING THE FINEST OF THE FINEST

I relished my role in training our new recruits. I always said we were creating the finest of the finest. And we did.

When we taught our recruits about radio procedures, we had them practice on a mock police radio we built using an intercom system. One of the instructors would be the radio operator sitting in his office with the base station, and the students were in the classroom where we had the head from one of our mobile radios used in the cruisers mounted. It operated just like the radios in the cars did.

Radios were not as common in the 1970s as they are today. It was a good training aid because when the students graduated from the academy, they could use the radio like a veteran officer.

We had physical fitness training every day. The academy was located on the fifth floor of the central police headquarters building, and the elevators were off limits for the recruits. The instructors exercised with them, so everyone was in shape when they graduated.

For years I was a jogger every night after work. I would do my mile run but most of the time it was two miles or more. I did this for several reasons. Exercise and weight control were the main reasons I started jogging. I jogged the first six blocks to warm up and ran after that. I reached a point where I felt guilty if I didn't get my run in. I bought a vinyl jogging suit with elastic on the neck, waist band, and sleeves of the shirt. The pants had elastic on the waist and cuffs. Wearing it was a lot like being in a steam bath the way it caused the sweat to pour out of me.

I lost the weight I wanted to so I shed the vinyl suit and continued to run. The weight stayed off and my endurance continued to build. I could go two miles without getting winded and my muscles were firming up. I felt good after I started running and I believe I am physically better off today because I stayed in shape all those years. On my nights off I jogged in the evenings and my sons would often run with me. This gave us some quality time together and they still mention it now and then.

Recruits were taught self-defense tactics and come-along holds.

When I was in the training academy, we had a very good physical fitness program and most of the people we trained stayed in shape through their whole careers.

Recruits were taught self-defense tactics and come-along holds as well as the proper use of the police baton and mace. There were no Tasers or stun guns at that time. Prior to the military draft ending, most of our recruits had been in the military. Now that the draft had ended, the pendulum swung the other way. Only one or two people in a class might have had prior military service.

Police officers still have a lot of parade duty when they are in uniform. When an American flag approaches, they must snap to attention and give the flag a military hand salute. They must know when and how to do it. One morning before roll call I told the instructor to teach them how to salute the flag when they are on parade duty.

I could hear their roll call from my office, then I heard open ranks, which is how I knew they were being inspected. I thought I would see how the salute was going. The class was at attention giving a three-finger salute to the flag just like their instructor was showing them. His two assisting instructors, both Navy veterans, were standing by with the biggest grins I had ever seen on their faces.

I had forgotten this instructor had not been in the military. When he came into the office to file the roll call roster, I said, "I didn't know you were a Boy Scout."

"How do you know I was?" he asked.

I must have grinned when I said, "In the military they salute with four fingers," and snapped him a salute.

He said, "I'll take care of that right away."

We were cleaning the gun range one morning when one of the instructors cut himself on something. It looked like it could use some stitches, so I told him I would drive him up to the hospital where the city had a contract to treat injured city employees.

"Find us a doctor who is sober."

We went to the emergency room, filled out some papers, and went into one of the examination rooms and waited for a doctor. We were sitting there when an inebriated person walked into the room and wanted to know how he can help us.

"Who are you?" I asked.

"The doctor on duty," he replied.

"You're drunk and you aren't touching this man," I said as I turned to the nurse, "Find us a doctor who is sober."

She told the doctor to come with her and they left.

She returned with another doctor who stitched up my colleague. The nurse said she was sorry she didn't know the doctor had been drinking when he came in, and she would make a report on it. I thanked her and said I would also be making a report.

If one of our recruits failed his morning inspection, we would have him (and a few women were among our ranks by now) do ten pushups right on the spot in front of the class. One time was all it normally took to have them make sure they were squared away at the next inspection. We seldom had anyone fail an inspection.

State law allowed a student to fail two weekly exams and still be certified if he or she re-took the exams and passed them. A recruit who failed a third exam was terminated. I formed study groups and even tutored them on how to take multiple choice tests. They all passed their makeup exams, but some failed their third exams and they had to be terminated.

We later discovered that even though some of our recruits had graduated from high school, they could not read at the grade level needed to answer many of the questions on our exams. The tests they took when they applied for the job needed to be adjusted so they would be able to meet the requirements of the job. I finally felt I was in a position to make a difference in the quality of police officers we had on the department. Our recruit class lasted thirteen weeks at that time. It took that long to cover all of the material they had to know when they went on the street with their coach.

One night during the recruit training class was called night patrol. The training staff would take the recruit officers on the street to observe the street officers on the "C" shift making actual calls.

We trainers tried not to become involved. This experience gave the recruits a break from the classroom and showed them what they would be doing once they were on the street. We went on a disturbance call in the parking lot of a bar. There were about thirty people in the lot and two police cars. Several people were fighting as the police were trying to break it up. One man in the crowd ran out and hit one of the officers in the back of his head. The officer was stunned but he didn't go all the way down.

The man turned and ran straight at us. We were in the dark shadows, and he didn't know we were there. He was close enough that I shoved him sideways when he ran by. It was enough to trip him up and he went head long into the side of a parked car. One of the officers ran up then and said, "I got him," and put the cuffs on him.

I heard one of the recruit officers say, "Goodie," as the man tripped and fell. I asked him later why he said "Goodie." He said because it was just like in the movies.

We had a busy night and I'm sure they had a lot to tell their fellow recruits the following day. They were all wound up when they went home for the night. Two recruits couldn't qualify with their revolvers and they were terminated. They sued. The court said the passing grade of seventy was arbitrary and ordered them reinstated with back pay. They both took the pay but neither of them came back to finish their training.

At one time the age for people to come on the police force was lowered from twenty-one to eighteen, not realizing a person had to be twenty-one to purchase ammunition. So some recruits went through the academy when they were eighteen before the age was raised back to twenty-one.

Once their classmates got to know them, there was some good-natured kidding about them needing a note from their mother so they could buy ammunition or they couldn't be in a bar after 9:00 p.m. even with their parents. Most of these young recruits retired with full pensions in their forties and moved on to high-dollar positions with other firms.

Height and weight requirements were eliminated as was the requirement that recruits could not be over a certain age when they came on the job if they passed the physical agility test, which had been approved by the courts.

They would be placed on the hiring list in the same order they finished the testing. In theory a person could be five feet tall, weigh 500 pounds, and be fifty-nine years old when hired; however, with the mandatory age limit of sixty, it would be a short career. We did have one older person who went through the academy and did well. He was promoted to sergeant in less than five years. He was an outstanding officer and a good person. He was diagnosed with terminal cancer and forced to take a non-service-connected pension. He passed away a short time after he retired.

We taught the first female who came on the job to become a sworn police officer.

Some exceptional people graduated from our academy while I was there. Three of them went on to become chiefs of police, six were deputy chiefs, four were captains, and there were many lieutenants and sergeants.

We taught the first female who came on the job to become a sworn police officer. We had women on the job prior to this, but they had not received the same training as the male officers did when they came on the job.

I was talking to an FBI agent one day about their agents with bachelor of science degrees in criminal justice. Before they started taking applicants with such degrees, the FBI only accepted applicants with law degrees. At first the people with the BS degree were looked down on by some agents with law degrees but that changed in time.

I was told by the agent in charge of this area at that time they would take all of our people who had the BS in criminal justice for two reasons. They had all passed a polygraph examination and they were sharp. The man saying this had a law degree, and yes the FBI did get a lot of our people. I was even recruited at one time for a federal position. I told them that I was honored they would ask but I was doing what I wanted to do now and didn't want to make a change. The FBI agent and I stayed in touch for several years after that.

After thirteen grueling weeks, the recruits were sworn in.

Our impressive graduation ceremonies were held in the auditorium at the police headquarters building. The recruits' families and guests would be there, and the recruits were all spit and polish in their new uniforms. The training staff always looked great too as they hurried about making sure nothing had been forgotten. Two of the instructors passed out programs at the door and two were seating the people. The news media were there.

The mayor and the safety director would wait in the chief's office with him and the deputy chiefs. When the phone rang, we knew the dignitaries were on their way. Everything was in place. The Training Commander was the master of ceremonies.

The recruits were seated in alphabetical order. The dignitaries were introduced and they said a few words. Then each recruit officer's name was called off and the mayor gave each of them their badge, shook their hand,

and congratulated them for their achievement. The safety director, chief, and deputy chiefs were all lined up in that order and also shook the recruit officer's hand and congratulated him or her.

This was followed by coffee and rolls, and the families pinning the badges on the new officers. The new officers were then excused for the day so they could spend some time with their families. They had their duty assignments and had already met their field training officers.

Their graduation banquet would take place that evening. It was a time for them to celebrate. The location for the banquet was chosen by the recruit officers. The only stipulation was that it had to be held in a party room at one of our upscale restaurants. One of the training staff took care of the reservations and acted as the treasurer. Everyone could bring a spouse or a guest, and this included the training staff and the dignitaries. The treasurer collected the money when the reservation was made.

The banquets were always a success. A brief time was taken to present achievement awards to the deserving recipients and the dignitaries were introduced again and asked to say a few words. Then the food was served. There was a cash bar after the meal and a good time was had by all.

The recruits were not the only ones who learned in the academy. We, the faculty, also learned more with each class we taught.

We used mug shots in some classes. One time one of the recruits reacted to a mug shot and said, "Hey that's my brother's old lady."

> His classmates think his sister-in-law is a prostitute.

This had never happened before and it never happened again while I was there. We convinced the recruit it was in his best interest not to say anything about the picture. It could hurt his family and they might turn against him so why chance it. We checked the picture out and it wasn't his sister-in-law after all. We told him he should engage his brain the next time before he opens his mouth. His classmates think his sister-in-law is a prostitute now and they always will.

The father of one of the recruits phoned us one morning and told us his son was in the hospital. He had suffered an appendicitis attack the night before, and his appendix had to be removed. The recruit was worried about what was going to happen to him now with the recruit class.

I knew one time before when a recruit couldn't complete the class they put him in the next class. I told the father I would find out. This was on a Thursday morning. The following Monday morning this young man was in the classroom. With an elevator pass he was able to graduate two weeks later with his class. He was one tough, determined young man.

I thought back when I came on the job. We had five weeks of training and it would have been less if our uniforms had come in when they should have. They finally sent us on the street in plain clothes in a cruiser with a uniformed officer. Our uniforms did come in two weeks later.

The officer I was working with was a former Marine. One night he was telling how all the women in the Marines were either lesbians or whores. In the next breath he was telling me he married one. I thought about asking him which one his wife was but I really didn't care, and I never thought that about female military personnel.

I said a little thank you to my maker when I came to work one night and learned he had been fired for stealing. The next man I worked with wasn't much better. The third officer was everything the first guys weren't. At last I was starting to learn something about police work, and I knew this man was not going to get me fired.

I was glad when the department went to a coach officer program for the recruits. It was so much better now than when I came on the job, but there was still a lot more that could be done to get the officer up to speed quicker. I wondered why it took so long to produce a viable police officer.

I began looking into the different programs and methods used by other departments. I heard about the San Jose California Field Training Officers Program and how well it was working for them. I knew other departments had used it as a model in designing their programs. The Traffic Institute at Northwestern University in Evanston, Ill., sent out their catalog and they were having a class on field training officers (FTO). The instructors were the police psychologist and captain from the San Jose California police department who designed and developed their FTO program.

I sent in a request to attend this class and it was granted. The first day of class I learned the instructors were staying at the same hotel I was. They asked me to join them for dinner. It was an invitation I could not refuse. One of our former officers was now on the San Jose department and they knew and liked him. I can't tell you what I had to eat that night, but I know I enjoyed myself. We had dinner together again and that time I picked their brains and learned a lot more about their FTO program than had been brought out in class. They gave me some extra sets of the textbooks.

When I returned home, I sent the class material to the chief with a note suggesting to him that I thought it was a good program that could be adapted to fit our needs. He sent back a short note: "Do it." Two of the training staff and I set out to do it and do it we did.

Using their model as a guide, we designed and developed the original FTO program for our department. We had five sets of the program printed and sent one copy to the chief with a short note attached: "Here it is. What is your opinion of it?"

About a week later the chief's secretary dropped it back off at my office and said the chief said to give this to you. A note on it said, "Good job. Implement with next recruit class."

When the next recruit class graduated, we had the field training program ready for them. We also had two command people who were very critical of the program. One was in a different bureau and had nothing to do with the program. I never figured out why he was so critical.

The program was a success. After six months these new officers had been taught and tested on every type of task they would be called on to perform. I'm sorry to say two of the officers did not make it through the program, but I was pleased to see the program worked. The new officers were working at the level of a two-year veteran even though they had only six months on the job. The criticism ceased after that.

The field training officers did a great job. I was proud of them, and I know they took pride in being an FTO. The program was established now so it was time for me to step out of the picture. Our academy, teamed with the FTO program, turned out some excellent officers. Some called them super cops.

Training staff in 1984 (from left), Ronald Goodrich, Mike Gordon, Dave Schlotman, Robert Dacus (seated), Don Osterhaus, and George Lynch.

Our instructors all received specialized training in the subjects they taught, and our in-service training was greatly improved over what it had been in the past. The training section even received recognition from the

Police Officers Association for the quality of the training they were receiving. All of our staff were professional instructors. The majority of them had been contacted with job offers from other agencies or schools.

In time we all went our separate ways by being promoted or moving to different jobs. Being able to transfer from one bureau into another was one of the benefits of the job that I really enjoyed. If for some reason an officer wanted a change and there was an opening, he or she could bid for it. I was in the training section for eight years—and I helped institute some massive changes. It was now time for me to make a change.

- Sixteen -

BONES MEETS CSI, OMAHA-STYLE

I transferred from being the Training Commander for police recruits to being the crime lab director in the spring of 1984. They were both administrative positions.

I had no desire to become a crime scene investigator. I was knowledgeable of what one did but being one was not my job. I was the last sworn officer to be the crime lab director. When I left in 1986, it became a civilian operation. The crime scene investigators were called I.D. technicians when I became the director.

I was able to purchase some new equipment for the crime lab while I was there. I remember when I tried to purchase some of that yellow plastic tape with the black lettering on it that says *POLICE LINE DO NOT CROSS.* My request was denied because it was too costly. Today you can see it everywhere.

One unusual case was a mummified body. A man had just purchased his home in 1984. It was a nice, well-kept older two-and-a-half-story house. He was in the basement when he noticed the door to another room in the basement had a padlock on it.

He got a pry bar and pulled the hasp off the door. It was dark in the room so he went upstairs to get a flashlight. He shined the light into the room, which appeared to have been a coal bin at one time. Then he made a discovery he will never forget.

There was a mummified body lying on the floor.

There was a mummified body lying on the floor. He called the police. The I.D. tech who investigated the crime scene phoned his supervisor and said he was unable to get any fingerprints. He thought he might be able to if he soaked the hands in some type of solution. The supervisor called me to see about having the coroner remove the mummy's hands.

The I.D. tech brought the hands into the lab where they were put in some fluid to soak. It worked. A copy of the prints was sent to the FBI lab in Washington, D.C., and the hands were returned to the morgue. The prints were not on file with the FBI, so we were back to square one.

The mummy was that of a white female. It was dressed in clothing like a younger person would wear. A wadded-up city bus transfer slip was found in one of the pockets of the jeans. The transit company was trying to find out when this transfer form was used.

I received a phone call from a woman who said she read in the paper about this body being discovered. She felt it had to be her friend who vanished years ago. I took down all of her information. She said the girl's mother was still living in town and had made a missing person report when her fourteen-year-old daughter had disappeared. She gave me the girl's name and the name of her mother.

I asked if she knew the name of the dentist her friend went to. She said no, but she would call the girl's mother and find out. I said, "When you call her, see if you can find out if the dentist still has her records and x-rays."

She called back in twenty minutes with the name of the dentist and said he still had her records and x-rays in the file. I thanked her and said I would give this information to the detective bureau. I made an information report and took it up to the bureau.

"I have a long shot for you," I told the detective as I handed him the report.

Bingo! The girl's dental records matched the teeth of the mummy. They now knew who she was and about when she died.

The detectives did some good work then. They checked with the person who owned the house at that time. He was able to give them the name of the person who was renting the house. They ran a check on the party and found he was serving time in Utah for rape. He had beaten a woman, raped her, and then left her for dead. The landlord made a positive ID on the man's mug shot from Utah.

The two detectives flew out to Utah to talk to the convict. They introduced themselves and one said to him, "You know why we are out here."

"Yes," he acknowledged. "It's about the girl I killed."

They advised him of his rights and he told them the whole story. I couldn't believe the way it all came to a close like it did. I don't know if the man will ever be released from prison in Utah, but if he is, Nebraska has a hold on him.

Someone had dumped a body down a secluded manhole years before.

Another unusual case was the surprising discovery made by a utility worker when he raised a manhole cover to climb down into it to do some repair work on the sewer near the airport. Someone had dumped a body down a secluded manhole years before. The utility worker found a complete skeleton.

The sunlight coming through the hole in the thick, metal manhole cover had bleached white round spots in the skull showing it had been there for a long time. The detectives thought this had to be the skeleton of a young woman who was murdered about three miles away from there, but her body had never been found.

Her killer had been convicted without a body because the evidence was so strong against him and was serving time for the crime. Her family had hired private investigators to find her body, and a psychic had them dig up a yard looking for her. Dental x-rays proved the skeleton was hers. Her family could finally have closure.

A construction crew was renovating a building next door to a mortuary in 1985. When they started to dig along the foundation wall facing the funeral home, they uncovered a lot of bones that appeared to be human.

So they stopped digging and called the police. We had them continue digging, and they uncovered several more bones. All of them were next to the foundation in a two-foot-wide by twelve-foot-long area about eight feet deep. It did not appear to be an Indian burial ground since there were no skulls, rib cages, or pelvis bones. There were only long bones from the arms or legs.

It appears they had to have been buried next to the foundation when the building was being built in 1944 and completely covered over when the foundation was back filled. Where the bones came from remains a mystery. I never heard what the experts had to say. There were a lot more questions here than there were answers.

During the time I was with the crime lab, Super Glue was being used to develop latent fingerprints on surfaces where they could never have imaged them before. Human skin is one good example. Computerizing fingerprints was in its infancy, and DNA was only being talked about. Technology in this field is changing so rapidly.

I attended a crime lab symposium at the FBI academy in Quantico, Va., and became acquainted with crime lab directors from different parts of the country. Only three of us there were sworn officers and we were older than most of the people there. I found the symposium to be very interesting and informative. I learned many things the week I was there and could see where we could make changes to improve our operation, and we did make some changes.

I tracked our I.D. techs when they made calls to process a vehicle for fingerprints when it was broken into. On the average it took one and one quarter hours from the time they left the lab until they returned to process a vehicle. Due to the porous finish on the interior of the cars, they seldom were able to lift a useable fingerprint. It was a waste of time and money to continue this nonproductive procedure so a change was made.

The officer taking the report would tell the people it is unlikely a useable fingerprint could be found in the car. If they wished to have their car checked for prints, they could make an appointment with the crime lab and bring their car down to the lab at central station and have it dusted. It would take about fifteen minutes to dust it. Few people brought their cars in to be printed, and we saved on the average of four wasted man hours every day. Over a year this was quite a sizable savings.

It was the worst cadaver he had ever seen or smelled.

One day it was getting close to lunch time, so I asked the supervisor where he would like to go for lunch. We were discussing it when one of the I.D. techs returned to the office from making a call. He said a man had been dead for a long time, and the blow flies had gotten to him. He said it was the worst cadaver he had ever seen or smelled. It made him sick and he had to run outside.

We laughed at him. He went across the hall to classify the man's fingerprints. Suddenly the stench reached us. When he opened his briefcase it was full of the smell of the cadaver from his last call. It filtered across the hallway into where we were and it was bad.

It started to gag us too, so to save face we took an early lunch. He was still laughing at us when we came back from lunch. It was hard to believe that much smell could have come from some papers in a briefcase that had been left open in the room with the deceased for such a short period of time.

One morning we received a call from the court. They were trying a burglary case and the burglar said he was innocent. He said it was his brother who broke into the place and the police had arrested him by mistake. The judge wanted someone to take the defendant's fingerprints to make sure they had the right party in court.

We sent a tech up to court to print one hand on the suspect and classify one finger and compare it to the suspect's fingerprint card. The tech showed it to the judge and explained it was a match. The judge asked the man if he had anything to say.

"Yes, your honor, I don't know how my brother got my fingerprints in the store."

The suspect was bound over to the district court for trial.

It was a slow afternoon when radio phoned the crime lab and said a cruiser found a dead woman floating in Carter Lake. It was a warm spring day. The I.D. tech asked me if I wanted to get some fresh air, so I rode along with him.

When we arrived at the scene, the body was out of the lake and the officer had covered it with an old plastic drop cloth. The officer meant well but he could have jeopardized the case by covering her with the dirty drop cloth. The I.D. tech slowly removed the drop cloth while being careful not to let anything drop off the cloth onto the body.

The body was that of a young white woman who did not appear to have drowned. The tech took photos of the crime scene. There were shoeprints and tire prints at the edge of the lake where the body was found. The prints showed where the car backed up to the lake and where someone had gotten out on the driver's side and walked to the rear of the car. There were a lot of shoeprints there, and they were deeper in the mud as if someone carried something heavy into the lake.

He put the camera away and was fingerprinting the body. He said, "Lieutenant, come look at this."

The sun shining on the body warmed it enough that bruises began showing on her neck and throat. She had been strangled and dumped in the lake.

He finished taking the fingerprints and took more pictures of the body and the bruises. The detectives were there now. The I.D. tech finished his investigation and briefed the detectives on what he found.

She had been strangled and dumped in the lake.

We returned to the crime lab, and he started to classify her prints. The following day we got a call from the detective bureau. They knew who the lady in the lake was and they were towing in her car from her apartment to have the crime lab go over it. The I.D. techs were not able to find any useable prints from the car, but there was a wet blanket in the trunk that they were letting dry, and they would send it in to the FBI lab when a suspect was found. They might be able to tie the two together. The tires on her car matched the tire prints at the lake.

When detectives arrested the suspect, his shoes matched the shoeprints at the lake. The suspect confessed to killing her while they were fighting over her cat. He said he put her body in her bathtub and filled it with cold water. After it was dark, he had wrapped the body in a blanket and put it in the trunk of her car. He drove down to the lake and dumped her body, drove home, and parked her car in front of the apartment building. He put her keys on the kitchen table in her apartment and pulled the door shut locking it. He hadn't bothered to mop up the water trail he made when he carried her wet dripping body out to the car.

We had a bad winter in 1962. It was cold and we had a lot of snow. Four teenagers slid off the road on the north side of the city during a blizzard and became stuck in the snow. They decided to stay in the car. When they were discovered the next day, they were all dead. They had been overcome by carbon monoxide gas, and they were all frozen stiff as boards.

There was no way they could be removed from the car. The car was towed to the county hospital and put in a heated garage. When the bodies thawed enough, they were removed from the car and taken into the morgue. What was sad about it all was that if they could have seen in the storm, they were less than fifty feet from a house where they could have found help.

Finding a frozen body was not all that uncommon when people heated their homes with coal. People would be overcome by coal gas and die. The fire would burn out and by the time anyone would check on them, they would be frozen solid.

When I was new on the job, I was on one of these calls. It was an elderly couple with a coal furnace. They were in bed in their night clothes. The furnace was out and it was freezing in the house. The newspapers on the porch had not been brought in for three days. They were both frozen solid. The coroner was there and he suspected coal gas. He left to find a telephone so he could call a mortuary to pick them up. When the mortuary people arrived, the coroner said, "They're frozen, but they are straight."

When we were back in the car, I asked my partner what the coroner meant when he said they were straight. He told me people die in different positions and they freeze that way making it very difficult to handle them. It sounded good to me.

In another unusual case a woman's body was found frozen in a creek in a secluded area of Hummel Park. Her head and upper body were submerged in the ice. Her lower torso and legs were sticking out of the ice exposed to the elements. She had to be chopped out of the ice, which was no easy task.

The body was taken to the county morgue where it could thaw out so an autopsy could be performed. The next morning when the morgue attendant arrived for work, he must have thought he would check to see if the body was thawing out. He pulled down the sheet she was under and saw her stomach move. They heard him scream just before he came running down the hallway and out the door.

He was never seen again.

Some nurses ran into the morgue to see what had scared the attendant so badly. Only the cadaver was there lying on the table. Just then some type of animal raised its head up from between the cadaver's legs and looked at them. More people screamed and ran down the hallway. Those people who did not run soon wished they had.

Just then some type of animal raised its head up from between the cadaver's legs and looked at them.

A skunk had been living inside the woman's frozen body for the winter. It had all it needed to survive. It had eaten its way into the body through the vaginal area. When the body started to warm up in the morgue, the skunk thought it was time to wake up. And when it saw all of the screaming people, it did what skunks do—sprayed the whole room. They closed the hallway door as quickly as they could, but it was too late.

It might as well have sprayed the whole hospital. Someone finally thought about raising the overhead garage door where they bring the bodies in and out of the morgue to let the skunk out. It worked. The critter left. But the smell stayed for a long time even after the area was treated.

Skunks don't hibernate for the winter, but they do sleep a lot unless they are disturbed and then they will wake up. The people at the hospital found that out. This skunk was apparently a meat eater. I was told most of the woman's intestines and internal organs had been eaten by something. I didn't understand why the skunk never came out when they were chopping the body out of the ice unless it was so cold it stayed in a deep sleep.

Vern Hauger at his farewell party given by crime lab personnel whom he called the OSS (Omaha's Super Sleuths), thus the bloodhound-themed cake.

- Seventeen -

FUNERALS, VOODOO, AND PANTY HOSE

I decided it was time for me to move on again. There was an opening for a lieutenant in the traffic section, and the crime lab was long overdue to have a civilian in charge. It was not cost effective to have a police lieutenant in charge when a civilian could do the same job for less money.

I enjoyed going back on the street in uniform again because I was at large in the whole city and the days went by so fast. I would just get to work and it was time to go home. We had a new police chief now. When our former chief retired, he said there would be a lot of politicking going on after he left and he was right. So far I had managed to stay out of it.

I was able to ride out the storm and it did pass. One of our United States Senators, the Honorable Edward Zorinsky, suffered a fatal heart attack when he and his wife were in town while they were attending a show put on by the Press Club. It so happened my captain had the next two days off. I knew the funeral would be large because the Senator was so well known and liked by so many people. The Senator was of the Jewish faith, which meant we had a lot of planning and preparation to do and not much time to do it in.

I called the captain thinking he might want to be advised. He just said, "You take care of it," and hung up the phone. I called the Jewish Funeral Home to find out when and where the funeral service and the interment would be. I called the funeral escort service to find out the route they would take from the synagogue to the cemetery. He suggested I lead the hearse using my red lights and follow him keeping my speed at 35 mph. I took a city map and marked every intersection where we would need an officer for traffic control.

Everything went as planned. I received a nice letter from Henry K. Giugni, Sergeant of Arms of the United States Senate for doing such a good job on short notice. I framed the letter and it now hangs on my home office wall. The real credit goes to the officers who directed the traffic and made the plan work.

The day shift traffic lieutenant's job (mine) had to be one of the best jobs in the department. I was on two personal injury accidents calls where rescue squads called for the life flight helicopters.

We lit up a landing area in a vacant lot with our headlights on our cruisers for one of them. It worked out well because the chopper pilot was good. The other one was in the daylight and the pilot was able to land in the roadway. One of the accident victims made it and the other one didn't.

HENRY KUUALOHA GIUGNI
SERGEANT AT ARMS

PHONE:
202-224-2341

United States Senate
OFFICE OF THE SERGEANT AT ARMS
ROOM S-321, THE CAPITOL BUILDING
WASHINGTON, DC 20510-7200

March 9, 1987

Lieutenant Vernard Hauger
Omaha Police Department
Traffic Section
505 South 15th Street
Omaha, Nebraska 68102-2769

Dear Lieutenant Hauger:

I would like to express my sincere personal appreciation for the assistance and support rendered to this office and the United States Senate during the recent funeral services for the Honorable Edward Zorinsky.

Despite the necessarily last-minute planning and preparation, the officers of the Omaha Police Department responded promptly, efficiently and in a manner worthy of the highest standard of public service.

I hope you will allow me the opportunity to repay, in part, my debt of gratitude by calling upon me whenever you are in Washington for assistance in organizing tours, securing passes or providing any other service required.

I know that Senator Byrd, our Majority Leader, joins me in expressing our gratitude for a job well done.

Again, many thanks. We owe you one.

Aloha,

Henry K. Giugni

HENRY K. GIUGNI
Sergeant at Arms

Commendation letter from the U.S. Senate.

I never realized the number of parades we have in the city each year until I went on the day shift of the traffic section and started working some of them. I was also surprised by the number of cross-country runs held here, which I never knew about. All of these functions were in addition to being responsible for enforcing the traffic laws.

During the 1970s a lot of construction of new buildings was going on in the city. Many of the older buildings were being demolished to make room for the new ones. They imploded most of the buildings during a time when there were fewer people and less traffic to contend with.

A little old homeless lady was seen running into one building about ten minutes before it was scheduled to be detonated.

When I was working traffic on the 3:00 p.m. to 11:00 p.m. shift, I was assigned to work at the building sites when the buildings came down. All traffic had to be stopped and the area had to be cleared. Everything had to be checked and rechecked.

One time a little old homeless lady was seen running into one building about ten minutes before it was scheduled to be detonated. They caught her right away but it still caused a one-hour delay.

Another time crews discovered someone had stolen some of the copper wire they put in to set off the charges, and it all had to be replaced. They had to make sure everyone was out and no one came in. The signal was given to set off the charges and implode the building. Then someone pushed the plunger on the hell box.

The buildings seemed to stand there when the first explosions occurred and then they sagged and dropped straight down. They reminded me of a pugilist who has just taken a blow to the head. He'll stand there for a split second and try to shake it off before going down. The building walls appeared to slip straight down, but when the debris hits the ground, the dirt and dust shoots out in all directions hugging the ground for blocks before it begins to rise up into the sky filling the air with black dust.

You don't want to be anywhere in this area when this happens. Once the air clears and you first see this pile of rubble standing there, it is hard to believe it was once a building. It is amazing they can drop a building this way. It can only be described as spectacular.

We also worked the fireworks shows each year. During the years I worked in traffic I only remember one accident. This was during a fireworks display at the Crossroads Mall, midtown. The sky rockets are fired out of tubes called mortars. They are set up in banks (rows), and each bank is loaded at the same time by one person. A second person lights the fuses.

If a rocket fails to fire, a new rocket is dropped on top of it when the bank is reloaded. When the fuses on this bank of rockets are lit, the one that did not ignite before should fire this time and both of them will shoot up into the sky and explode at about the same time.

There was a new man on the crew one July Fourth. This was his first night on the job. He was loading a bank of mortars. When he bent over to load one on top of one that had not fired before, it shot out of the mortar hitting him just below his shoulder. Some of the crowd who witnessed his arm going end over end through the air saw something they will never forget.

Some of the crowd who witnessed his arm going end over end through the air saw something they will never forget.

One of the traffic officers saw it happen, and he took off his military-type web belt and put it around the stump of what was left of the man's arm and pulled the belt up tight with its roller belt buckle shutting off the blood. He called radio on his portable radio and asked for the rescue squad. He came through clear. He told them what he had, where he was, and how to get there among the thousands of people in attendance.

We heard the squad coming and saw it go on down the street past us. We had no way of calling them. He contacted radio again and told them he thought the rescue squad was going the wrong way and gave them direction on how to get to him. They came right to us then.

They showed the directions radio gave them. Someone wrote them down wrong. They took the man's arm with them, but they were not able to reattach it.

I enjoyed working these different events and having front row seats was great. Sometimes it could be a real pain getting the people out of the parking lots and back on the streets after an event, but it usually went fast and we looked forward to working the event again.

We worked crowd control or traffic control for most of the larger functions in the city. We met a lot of people. Some of them were important people and some of them thought they were important. Fortunately for us there were more good people than there were bad ones. Unfortunately for us we tend to remember the bad ones longer.

I recall one parade we worked was part of an ethnic festivity held each year. The streets were blocked off for a carnival with all of the rides, shows, and games. It was a hot day when the parade was over, so we took a break and were having a soda.

We were back in service now and could be reached by radio if we were needed for a call. Some of us had not even ordered our drinks yet when this gentleman came over to us and started yelling he wasn't paying us to stand around and drink pop. I thought to myself where did he escape from. I told him to calm down but he wasn't listening to me.

People were stopping now to see what was going on. I told him if he didn't calm down, we were going to arrest him. He heard that and calmed down. I asked who he was and he said he was a board member of the organization putting on this event.

He said they were paying lieutenant (blank) X number of dollars to provide security for them. I told him the lieutenant he named had nothing to do with us. We were on-duty officers who worked the parade and we were going to have a cool drink and leave.

I said, "You should contact the lieutenant you have the contract with to provide your security and find out where they are before you jump on the first uniform you see. Your actions are uncalled for and you owe us an apology."

He didn't say a word, just turned and walked away.

I was leaving when I saw the head of their board. I had worked with him before. I told him I had a problem and wanted to talk to him. I explained everything that happened and told him I was going to make a full report to my chief.

He said, "That won't be necessary. I'll take care of it."

We all received a letter of apology from the board member. Apparently the board member was one of those people who thought he was important. The traffic crew was made up of exceptional officers. They were all professional people who knew what their job was and they all did it very well.

We were in court one afternoon when an older man was contesting a speeding ticket. He suddenly leaned backward, then straightened up, and fell forward hitting his head on the judge's bench as he collapsed on the floor. He was not breathing and he didn't have a pulse. Someone said should we start CPR.

I turned on my portable radio and called for a rescue squad. It only had to come from half a block away. The date was August 9, 1972, and the judge was the Honorable Paul J. Hickman. He wrote a letter to our chief commending us for the way we handled the situation.

The judge ordered the courtroom cleared and had the people go into an adjoining courtroom. I heard the rescue squad leave the fire station, and I told one of the officers to take the elevator to the first floor and hold it for the rescue squad people.

With the CPR, the man had a pulse now, but he wasn't breathing on his own. The squad people put a breathing device over his mouth and nose with a squeeze ball on it. One of them worked the squeeze ball while the other two loaded him on a gurney, and they were on their way to the hospital. The people returned to the courtroom. The judge gave them a short talk praising the way we took charge of the situation and the trials resumed.

The court cases seemed to be moving faster than they were before the man suffered his heart attack. Most of the people were now pleading guilty. Somehow the heart attack victim managed to hang on for seven more days before he passed away. I believe we did the right thing in trying to save him even though his last days were a struggle.

They discovered he was wearing cut-off women's panty hose.

One of the motorcycle officers had to lay his bike down when a truck came out from a side street right in front of him without stopping. He slid on the pavement and had some nice burns. When they cut his clothing off, they discovered he was wearing cut-off women's panty hose under his underwear. He explained that some of the police motorcycle officers wear them because they perspire so badly riding the motorcycle in their hot riding breeches, they break out in a bad rash and become raw. They help keep them dry and the rashes aren't as bad.

One of the nurses at the hospital asked me if this was true. I told her I didn't know but I would find out. I told her that at roll call the next day I would have the motorcycle officers drop their drawers and we will see if it is true.

She flushed a little and said, "You can't do that, can you?" I had to chuckle then.

I asked the guys and some said they wore them and they also used a medicated powder. They said they didn't get a rash if they used the two together. They didn't know it then but the panty hose acted as a barrier between their skin and the wet, coarse riding breeches preventing them from rubbing against the skin and causing the rash. Today they manufacture undergarments designed for the bike riders, which replaced the panty hose.

I was surprised when I first learned there are believers in voodoo among the black residents of our city. I had heard about the voodoo dolls with the pins stuck in them casting spells on people, but I just spaced it off until I made calls where black people discovered gray powder or ashes on their porches or across their doorways into their homes. Wax spots where candles were burned or piles of twigs or chicken bones were common.

I have no idea what any of this meant, but I do know some of the people were really afraid when they saw it or if any of this happened to them. An older black man told me voodoo spells were cast on these people for different reasons, and they can be very powerful if one believes in it.

There have been calls where witchcraft was suspected, but I have never made one. I know nothing about witchcraft. Sometimes ignorance is bliss, and I intend to stay that way. I know witchcraft is practiced in our city, but I have no desire to learn anything about it.

I recall one time when they suspected witchcraft when there was evidence that a group had gathered one night in a secluded area in the city and had a huge fire. Evidence showed they danced around the fire and someone had sacrificed a black cat. I believe most people would agree this was a rather bizarre thing to do no matter who did it.

- Eighteen -

GUNFIRE—OFFICER DOWN

I was still new on the job when I made my first "help an officer call." This turned out to be a traffic arrest that went bad. The party who was arrested was being followed to the police station by the arresting officer. Instead of turning left to go to the police station, as he had been told, he went straight ahead going over the Missouri River bridge into Council Bluffs, Iowa.

The arresting officer gave chase and notified radio of his direction of travel. Our radio operator was relaying this information to the Council Bluffs police. The next transmission our officer made was when he had the vehicle stopped and gave their location.

A few seconds later a second officer called radio from the same location and said they needed a rescue squad. The suspect had shot both of them, and he had shot the suspect. A "help an officer call" was put out then. This all happened during shift change.

Officers from both shifts responded. We beat the rescue squad. One officer was lying by the suspect's car with his gun belt on the ground beside him. The suspect was lying in the intersection on his back about fifty feet away from him, and the other officer was lying across the street away from both of them.

My partner sent me to the intersection one block away and had me detour all the traffic except for the rescue squad. We closed off the whole area around the crime scene and assisted the Council Bluffs police wherever they wanted us. The suspect was dead and the car he was driving was a stolen vehicle.

One of the officers was paralyzed from the arms down, and the other one had disabling internal injuries. Neither would work again.

The second "help an officer call" I was on was a stick-up at a bar. The suspect was running from the bar when he ran into a plain-clothes detective and a gun battle followed.

The detective had fired his last round, and the suspect was running toward him to shoot him before he could reload. A cruiser pulled up then. The suspect decided to shoot the cruiser officer instead of the detective and hit him in the buttocks.

Then a sheriff's deputy arrived and shot the suspect, hitting him in the forehead centered above his eyes. We drove up in time to handcuff the suspect and transport him to the hospital. He was real lucky the shot hit the front of his skull and did not penetrate it. Instead it followed the skull up and over the top of his head where it exited the back of his head.

The suspect was really bad-mouthing the police in the emergency room when the doctor was working on him. The doctor started to pack the wound with the yellow antibiotic gauze they use. He packed a whole roll in and tied another onto it and packed it in. He quit after the third roll. The man's head looked several hat sizes larger. The doctor told us the gauze would have to come out in a week. I learned some time later the doctor's father was a retired police officer.

My third "help an officer call" was a real mess. During the winter three men stuck up a grocery store and someone inside the store had pushed the hold-up alarm. The cruiser arrived as the stick-up men sped away. They started shooting at the cruiser as they turned into a residential area. A short time later they lost control of their car and it spun out. The running gun battle continued on foot through the neighborhood.

I arrived as officers were arresting one of the suspects who had been found hiding in some bushes. They pointed the direction the others went. I went around the house into the backyard. The rescue squad was there working on a police officer who had been shot.

The body of a white man was there too. It was snowing hard now. I heard some yelling in the front yard of a house, which was directly behind the yard I was in. I went around the house and found another man in cuffs sitting there. His face was covered with blood from a wound on his head. Another body was by the street.

His face was covered with blood from a wound on his head.

I saw the cruiser sergeant was there and asked if they still needed me. He said, no, everything is under control. I said I'll catch you later.

Before it was over, though, we had one officer shot, one Good Samaritan killed, one bad guy arrested, one bad guy shot and arrested, and one bad guy killed.

During my fourth and last "help an officer call," I was the one who needed help. I was working on a special assignment and had left a business building and was walking across their parking lot to my car when I noticed a cruiser was parked facing me on a side street about a quarter of a block away.

A man with his back to me was walking toward the cruiser. He could not have been more than ten feet away from it. I saw him drop whatever he had in his arm and point a hand gun at the office sitting in the cruiser. He fired two rounds and started running down the street away from me.

I used my portable radio and put out the first and only "help an officer call" I ever made. I ran across the street to see how badly the officer was shot. He had not been hit but he was in a state of shock.

The district sergeant then called for the rescue squad to come to a location less than two blocks away from us. Radio asked him the nature of the call. He said, "I just shot the party on the help an officer call."

The whole thing was over in less than five minutes. He said he heard the help call and the party ran around the corner in front of him with the gun still in his hand.

He knew the man was wanted for the robbery of a Quik Shop no more than thirty minutes before. He jumped out of his car, drew his service revolver, and dropped the man. The only reason he hadn't shot at the sergeant was because his gun was jammed from shooting at the officer. The officer had been at lunch when the stick-up happened, and I was working on a different radio channel so neither of us knew about the robbery. The suspect survived his wounds.

We received an attempted armed robbery call. The victim shot the suspect and the rescue squad was en route. We were met by an older man dressed in a suit who handed my partner a pistol. He said he was walking down the sidewalk going to church when he met the suspect walking toward him.

When they were about to meet, the suspect pulled a hunting knife out of his waistband and said, "Give me your money, old man."

The old man drew his .38-caliber pistol out of his right front pocket and fired two shots pointblank at the robber.

So the old man drew his .38-caliber pistol out of his right front pocket and fired two shots pointblank at the robber. The suspect dropped his knife and turned running back down the street away from him. The knife and two spent cartridges were lying on the sidewalk.

The old man said, "The guy is dead," as he pointed down the sidewalk about a half block.

The squad arrived and we showed them where the suspect was. My partner stayed with the victim and called for the crime lab for pictures and measurements. I walked down to where the squad was. I only walked a short distance when I saw a blood trail on the sidewalk, and it got worse as I got closer to the suspect. It was now a bloody mess where he was lying.

The squad captain said one of the bullets hit his femoral artery and he bled out. They transported the body to the county hospital where the autopsy would be done. My partner called the detective bureau and told them what we had and what we had done so far. They said when the crime lab is done with their investigation to bring our reports and the victim into them and they would do the follow-up.

Another time, I was going to the assembly area when a call came out on an auto/fixed object personal injury accident. We were to advise if rescue squad was needed. I was only a block and a half away so I told radio that I would advise on the squad. The car had hit a tree (thus, the fixed object), and the driver was slumped over the steering wheel.

I ran over to check on him. He had been shot in the head. The bullet entered his head on the left side just in front of the top of his ear and exited the right side of his head. He was still alive. I advised radio to send the rescue squad.

The command cars had mobile phones in them, so I contacted the detective bureau and told them what we had. They advised they were sending a car out and to have the cruiser meet them at this address. It was about a hundred yards down the street. The rescue squad took the party to the hospital.

The cruiser arrived and I briefed them, and they went down the street to meet the detectives. The accident investigator arrived and I filled him in and saw the detective car arrive and the cruiser officers get out of their car. They called for me to meet them. I drove up to them and they briefed me. The man who had done the shooting was in the house. The cruiser officers watched the outside of the house while the detective and I knocked on the front door.

The man who lived in the house answered the door and had us come in. He said when he came home he found the man who was shot in bed with his wife. He said when he went to get his gun both the man and his wife ran out of the house.

He got his gun and ran after them. He saw the man get into a car. He ran over to the car just as the man started the engine and pulled the shift lever into drive. He pointed the gun at the man's head and shot twice. He said the car accelerated at full throttle until it ran into the big maple tree down the street. He didn't see where his wife went.

He went back into the house and waited for us because he knew we would be coming there pretty soon. The wife was the one who had called in the shooting. The cruiser officers took the suspect into the police station. The accident investigator finished up. The crime lab came out and the detective left to interview the wife and finish his investigation.

I shined the spotlight on him and he didn't move.

After a busy night, we were parked by the police call box at the end of our shift waiting to be called in. I caught my daily report up and I was ready to call it a night, but instead radio gave us a call of a shooting.

When we arrived on the call, there were no lights on in the house, and a man was sitting in the yard. He was a huge person; he had to weigh well over 400 pounds. I shined the spotlight on him and he didn't move. He looked like a statue of Buddha. He had three blood spots on the front of his pink shirt.

I got out of the car and walked up to him. I gave him a quick check. I didn't find any vital signs. He was dead.

Somehow when he died, his arms wedged in such a way they held him in a sitting position. A woman came out of the house next door. She said she thought she heard shots and she looked out of her back door in time to see her neighbor man come out of his back door onto the stoop and hurry down the three steps to the sidewalk. He stopped there, grabbed his chest, and dropped straight down in a sitting position.

She said she used her wall phone by the door to call the police and she watched until we came. No one had come out of the house so the shooter must still be inside. We called for backup to watch the outside of the house while we went in to find the shooter.

The rescue squad took the shooting victim away.

My partner yelled, "Police. Is anyone in there?"

What sounded like a man answered, "Yes, I'm in the basement."

My partner said, "Come up here. We want to talk to you."

He said, "I'll be right up," and the lights came on. An elderly man who looked to be in his late seventies came up the stairs.

My partner patted him down and asked, "Where's the gun?"

The man said, "Downstairs in my tool box."

We retrieved a Charter Arms, .25-caliber, semi-automatic pistol. Three empty cartridges lay on the floor. The man told us he was the owner of the house and the shooting victim was his renter. He was behind in his rent by two months and refused to pay him, so the old man came over and was in the process of cutting off his power when the renter came home.

He said the man came down the stairs cursing at him. The renter said he was going to kill the old man, so he reached in his tool box and pulled out his gun and told the man he better stop.

The Buddha-sized renter continued to come at him.

The old man shot him once, but it didn't slow him down so he shot again, but the man still came at him. He fired the third time. He said the man stopped, looked at him, and turned back up the stairs and out the back door.

The old man said he was going to take the circuit breaker out before the renter returned. He heard the sirens and knew there was no need for him to hurry.

We phoned the detective bureau and they said to handle the call and bring the suspect in to them. We called the crime lab for measurements and pictures. We finished our reports and took the arrest into the bureau and turned the evidence into property.

It was after 2:00 a.m. when I went to bed that night. I was beat and I went right to sleep. I woke up with a start. I dreamed of the dead man sitting there looking out into space. This had never happened to me before, but I had always had time in the past to unwind with other calls before I went home and went to bed. This never happened to me again. We never went to court on this case. The old man may have been allowed to plea bargain.

When I was working days, I was right on top of a shooting call when I received it. I pulled over to the curb and went up to the house. It was one of those big old houses that had been converted into apartments.

The front door was standing open, and just inside an older woman was on the floor cradling the head of a young woman in her arms. She had been shot in the back of the head. The bullet came out of her forehead just above her left eye.

A young man in an Army uniform was also lying on the floor. He had been shot in the right temple. His head was turned so that each time his heart beat the blood shot up into the air like Old Faithful in Yellowstone National Park. There was less blood with each heart beat until it stopped.

There was nothing we could do.

I picked up a revolver from the floor. It had been fired twice. The rescue squad arrived and were tending to the woman. They took both of them to the hospital. I asked the older woman what happened.

She said there was a knock on her door from the young woman who lived upstairs. She wanted to use the phone to call the police. Her husband had come home from Vietnam, and she told him she had met a new guy while he was gone and she wanted a divorce. She said he went crazy and started dumping his duffel bag on the floor and throwing things around, so she came down to call the police.

The woman said the man came down the stairs and walked up behind the young woman and shot her in the back of her head and then he shot himself.

I called the detective bureau and told them what I had. They asked me to make the reports. With the help of the lady on the first floor I was able to get the information I needed to complete the reports on both parties. I locked their apartment and asked the lady who lived downstairs if she had a mop and a bucket. I said I would try to clean up some of the bloody mess in the hallway for her. She thanked me and said she would take care of it.

I went to the hospital. Both husband and wife were DOA, and their bodies were sent to the county morgue for autopsies. I turned the evidence (revolver, two spent cartridges, and four bullets) in to the property room.

A year later I received a subpoena to appear in a civil court hearing to determine whose family—his or hers—received the inherence of their estate. The court ruled since there was no will in force, when the husband died before his wife, his property went to her, so when she died, her property went to her family.

- Nineteen -

FROM TRAGIC TO THE BIZARRE: KIDS AND DOGS AND CRAZIES

When I was still new on the job in January 1960, we received a radio call of an auto-pedestrian personal injury accident. The rescue squad and accident investigator were en route. We arrived on the call before they did.

It had been a long cold winter with a lot of snow. The snow plows had created a large ridge row of snow against the curbs of the street. A small boy six or seven years old had been standing on the ridge with several other children waiting for the traffic signal to change to green so they could cross the street.

Suddenly his feet slipped on the ice-packed snow ridge and he shot feet first into the traffic lane under a passing truck. Both of his legs were fractured below the knees when the rear tires ran over them. If he had slipped a second sooner, his body would have been crushed.

A woman was trying to console him. The boy said he had to go home. His mother was going to be mad. Some of the children had gone to get her because the family lived just a block away. I told the little boy I would talk to his mother and she wouldn't be mad. I told him he would have to go to the hospital and we would bring his mother there. He seemed to calm down.

The rescue squad was leaving with the boy as his mother arrived. We told her what happened and said he had two broken legs. I told her he was so afraid she would be mad at him.

"I said I would talk to you and you wouldn't be," I told the mother.

The accident investigator said he would take the mother to the hospital and finish up his report. We hit back in service on the radio. As serious as the boy was injured, he was lucky. It could have been a lot worse.

It is one of the worst calls a police officer will ever make.

That summer I made my first investigation of a sudden infant death. The mother had put her two-month-old baby in bed and when she checked on it twenty minutes later, the baby was dead. Cause of death was SIDS—Sudden Infant Death Syndrome. When no cause of death can be found, it is ruled SIDS. There is no obvious cause for it and it is not generally preventable or contagious. It just happens and it is one of the worst calls a police officer will ever make.

It was about 6:00 p.m. and I was headed for the restaurant to eat my supper. I wanted to eat before 7:00 and beat the rush of calls we would get every night beginning then and continuing on through most of the shift. If you didn't eat before then, you might not get a break.

I didn't make it that night. I received a call to make an investigation. This type of call means a death is involved. The address was to an apartment building. The apartment was on the second floor. I rang the doorbell and a man answered. I followed him into a bedroom. A woman wearing a slip was sitting on the bed holding a small baby in her arms with its face pressed against her.

Blood was all over the front of her slip. The man said he picked up his wife from work when she got off and they picked up their baby from the day care. Then they stopped at the laundry to pick up their dry cleaning on their way home. He said he placed the dry cleaning on the bed, and she laid the baby on the bed next to it. She took off her coat and hung it up and then she pulled her dress up over her head and took it off. She noticed her baby had turned over and was face down on the plastic laundry bags their dry cleaning came in.

She dropped her dress and grabbed the baby to pick it up. The dry cleaning bag came up with the baby. The bag was stuck to its face. It was sucked into the baby's nose and down in its mouth. He tried to pull it loose but it tore. It was still blocking the baby's nose and throat. She was able to tear a hole in the bag and pull it out of the baby's throat. They tried to breathe in the baby's mouth, but frothy blood came out of its mouth when they did.

> It was too late.
>
> The baby was gone.

They called the rescue squad, but it was too late. The baby was gone. The squad called us, and I called the coroner. He was going to send someone out to pick up the baby so an autopsy could be done. I explained everything to the parents so they would know why everything was being done.

I had never seen a suffocation before. I didn't realize the veins can rupture and cause the bloody foam. This was one of the worst calls I had to make. I stayed with the parents for a while after the coroner had picked up the baby. I didn't have a meal break that day, but I wasn't hungry.

Drowning was another tragedy. I had a drowning where an eighteen-month-old baby fell into their swimming pool and drowned while the mother was busy in the house entertaining a neighbor. Her husband rushed home from work while I was interviewing her. He was very upset because I was talking to her then. He got loud and said he thought I could wait. I told him I could do it here or I could take her downtown and do it. I asked him which way he wanted me to do it.

He left the room and I finished my report. I contacted one of the county attorneys I had worked with before and asked if I should arrest the mother for child neglect. He said for me to send copies of my report to him and he would charge her if he thought we had a case. He thought it would be better if he swore out a warrant later.

I investigated a felonious assault case where a man caused his own daughter's death when he was assaulting her mother. I charged him with two counts of felonious assault, and when the daughter died, the county charged him with manslaughter for her death.

The family kept calling me. They didn't understand why he was charged with manslaughter for killing his daughter when it was an accident and he didn't mean to do it. I told them to ask the county attorney. I had nothing to do with the charges. I was glad when he was finally found guilty and sentenced. Then the family stopped calling me.

Some cases I wish I could forget, but I never will, and I won't go into detail here. One was a two-year-old girl who was raped by her mother's live-in boyfriend, and another was a baby that was killed by her father with a hammer.

In the thirty years I worked on the job I never reached a point where it didn't bother me when I made a call where children were injured, sick, or dead.

We received a dog bite call in one of the more affluent areas of the city. The address was to a large three-story brick home. When we arrived on the call, we were met by a woman in her late thirties who said, "Hurry this way." We followed her into the house going through a great room into a second room where a cherry-wood staircase went up to a mezzanine enclosed by a cherry-wood railing.

A boy who appeared to be about ten years old was lying face down on the floor at the foot of the stairway in a pool of blood. A large black and tan Doberman Pinscher was attached to his right leg above his knee.

The dog's eyes were closed, and it refused to let go of the boy's leg.

She said the boy was her son. He was walking down the stairs when he fell letting out a yell and that's when his dog attacked him. The dog's eyes were closed, and it refused to let go of the boy's leg.

I told her I thought I could choke the dog and get it to release the boy, but I didn't know what we would do with the dog then. She indicated pocket doors on both sides of this room we could close and keep the dog inside. She slid the doors closed on the far side of the room and closed one of them on our side.

She said, "Once the dog releases him, we can get out this way and shut the door."

"You get the boy out of the room when the dog lets loose of him, and my partner and I will be right behind you. We will have to get the door closed in a hurry," I said.

My partner took hold of the dog's collar with both hands. The boy was wearing a military-type web belt with a slide buckle on it. I put his belt around the dog's neck and drew it down as tight as I could holding the buckle with my other hand. I told my partner not to let go.

The dog let loose of the boy's leg then and started to fight us. The boy's mother pulled the boy out of the room. My partner and I held onto the dog. Suddenly it went limp and we pulled it over close to the door before we released it. We got out of the room as fast as we could and closed the door.

The boy's leg was really torn up. The muscle was ripped apart and five inches of it was torn loose from the bone. We called the rescue squad for the boy and the Humane Society for the dog. The dog was now up and running around the room wondering what it had done.

We stopped to see how the boy was doing a few days later. He had been in surgery for six hours, but things looked good. He was going to be fine except for a nasty scar on his leg. They had put the dog to sleep because they couldn't take the chance of it doing something like that again.

We received a call about a seven-year-old boy who had put a crayon in his nose and his mother was unable to get it out. I looked up his nose with my flashlight and sure enough he had an orange crayon in there. I asked if she had any tweezers. I thought I could get it out and save her a trip to the hospital.

She said already tried but the tweezers were not wide enough to go over the crayon. I asked her if I could bend them to fit. She said yes. I spread them wider apart and bent the ends of them closer together.

I put the tweezers into the boy's nose and took hold of the crayon and pulled it out about a quarter of an inch. I told him I wanted him to hold still. I said I was going to count to three and try to pull it out. I asked him if he was okay and he said yes. I said one and almost pulled it out. I said two and pulled it out. Then I said three and here it was—almost three inches long.

The boy promised me he would put his crayons in the box and not in his nose.

Another boy caught his knee between the balusters holding up the handrails on the staircase in their home. His mother had tried all sorts of different lubricants on his knee hoping to free him. The only thing she managed to do was make his knee swell up so it was an even tighter fit.

We told her we might have to saw one of the balusters out, but we would try to spread them far enough apart to free him first. We figured one of the balusters might break when we tried to spread them apart.

She agreed to let us try it. We lifted the boy so his knee was centered in the baluster between the top and the bottom of them and had his mother hold him there. He was close enough to the bottom of the staircase so we could stand on the floor and reach the balusters. I grabbed the balusters on each side of his leg below his knee and my partner did the same thing above his knee.

We pulled at the same time. She pulled her son out as the balusters gave enough to free him.

I recall one embarrassing moment when I was serving traffic warrants. I stopped at a house and saw a sign posted on the front that said in very bold letters: BEWARE OF DOG. When I got out of the car, a little dog came running around the side of the house barking at me. I was watching the dog as I started to open the storm door on the front porch. I didn't want it to nip my heels.

When I opened the door, a very large German shepherd on the porch stuck its head in my face showing his teeth as he growled at me. I slammed the door shut on its neck and head holding him there. He really made some noise then.

A man came out of the front door and demanded, "What the hell is going on?"

"I have a warrant for Raymond Foster."

He said no one by that name lives here. I advised him to get his dog. He got the dog and I closed the door. I thanked him and left. When I was safely in the car, I looked at the warrant. I was at the wrong address.

Something different happened every day on this job, which made it so unique. No two days were the same. It was impossible to become bored.

Two nude white females driving downtown in a convertible with the top down

I received a call one day to check the report of two nude white females driving downtown in a convertible with the top down. One was a blond and the other was a redhead. There was no description of the car, so the call must have been legitimate. Everyone was looking at the women and they didn't see the car. I checked the area but I never found them.

We did have a nude white male in his twenties downtown one morning. He was on his way to Washington, D.C., to meet Natalie Wood in front of the Washington monument. God told him to take off all of his clothing so she would recognize him. He had to meet her in forty minutes. We transported him to the county hospital for a mental evaluation.

We had another nude male in his fifties who painted himself with a silver-blue-colored mixture of paint and who knows what else mixed in a five-gallon bucket. He was in the process of painting a storefront when we arrived on the call. He was painting the window glass and all.

We asked him what he was doing. He said he had this wonderful liquid and he was told to put it on this building and it would be made new again. We asked who told him to do it and he said the voice did. We asked him if the voice told him to paint himself.

"Yes," he said, "it is going to make me young again."

"It might make you sick," I suggested.

"No, it won't. It's good," and he drank some of it before we could stop him.

He instantly became very sick and regurgitated it. He fell to the ground in a fetal position and laid there in much pain. We called the rescue squad and they transported him and the bucket to the hospital.

In the summer of 1961 I had a crime against property report, which had to be approved by the detective bureau captain. Someone had stolen six bed sheets from a clothesline where they had been hung up to dry after being washed. All crime against person and property reports had to be approved by the detective bureau captain then.

The captain asked me what color the bed sheets were. I didn't know. He was one of the people who had to give everyone a hard time. He wanted to know how I expected them to find the sheets if they didn't know what color they were.

I said, "I don't."

He came unglued and screamed, "What did you say?"

You could almost see the steam coming out of his ears.

"You asked me how I thought they could find the sheets without knowing what color they were. I said I don't know how anyone could possibly find them without knowing what color they were," I replied.

He stammered and said, "You find out what color they were."

I phoned the reporting party and found out.

I wrote, "The sheets were white," on the last line on the report. I took it back up to the captain and he signed it without saying a word. I thanked him for catching my mistake. I said we both would have looked pretty stupid if he hadn't caught it. He didn't say anything. I said I would be more careful with my reports and left.

I knew he would call the reporting party to see if I had contacted him to find out the color of the sheets. There was no doubt in my mind that he would check to see if I had called the person. I knew the next report I had to have him sign better have all the t's crossed and the i's dotted.

It was about dusk one summer evening when we received a call about someone acting suspicious in a school parking lot. We were nearby. When we turned into the school, we noticed a car in the lot with its trunk lid raised parked near the back of the lot. At that time we saw a man at the rear of the car duck down behind it.

We stopped in front of the car and walked back to the rear of it. We were surprised to find a man dressed in a bra and a half-slip hiding there. He was shaking like a leaf and he was scared to death. We asked him what

> We were surprised to find a man dressed in a bra and a half-slip hiding there.

he was doing there and he said changing clothes. He had two women's wigs in the trunk and an open suitcase containing female clothing plus a makeup case and some shoes. We asked him for some identification, and he took a billfold out of a pair of trousers lying in the trunk. He was who he said he was and he owned the car.

We ran a records check and he wasn't wanted for anything. He said he liked to wear women's clothes. We asked him why he didn't dress at home. He said his wife didn't know he was doing this and begged us not to tell her.

We told him it wasn't our job to tell wives their husbands like to run around in drag and do whatever one in drag does. We told him to get dressed and to find another place to change clothes. We made out an information report on him and he left dressed as a man.

One fall night around 9:30 we were driving through a residential area when we observed a person on the front porch of one of the houses. The person's back was to us and the suspicious person was looking in one of the front windows of the house, with hands cupped on the sides of the face to see in the window.

We pulled over to the curb and parked. We were quiet when we shut the doors and walked up on the porch behind the person. The person was so intent in looking in the window, we were able to stand there for a minute before my partner said, "What do you see?"

The person jumped and turned around. Our Peeping Tom was a woman. The porch light came on and a man stuck his head out and said, "What's going on?"

"Police. Do you know this woman?"

He looked, "I sure do. I have a restraining order on her and there is a warrant for her arrest. She has been stalking me for years, and she always manages to avoid being arrested."

She was becoming a bit unruly so we handcuffed her. He said he had a copy of the restraining order and it had the judge's seal on it. We called to check on the warrant and it was on file. We towed her car in for safekeeping and arrested her for the warrant and also booked her for contempt of court for the violation of the restraining order.

We received a radio call to the bus station about a transient panhandling the people waiting for the bus to arrive. The agent pointed out the party to us. He was now sleeping on one of the benches. I knew better but I still took a hold of his shoulder with my right hand and shook him while I told him to wake up.

That was a mistake. He had ahold of my thumb now and he was twisting it backward. I heard it pop and boy did it hurt. I hit him with my stick using my left hand, but he held on. My partner gave him a couple of shots with his stick and the guy turned my thumb loose. We were able to handcuff him and take him to jail.

After he was booked I went to the hospital. My thumb was dislocated. They put it back in place and taped me up, putting a metal guard over my thumb. They gave me some pain pills and told me to see the city doctor in a week.

I worked inside for two weeks after that. I was back on street duty a week after that. This was the only job-related injury I had.

One night when I was working with a rookie officer, we were in foot pursuit of a man. We were running between the houses through the yards. I was in the lead then and my partner was close behind. As I went past the rear of a house, I thought I heard a dog growl and then I heard my partner scream.

I let the party go and went back to see what happened to my partner. The bad guy and I must have awakened the dog when we ran past his dog house. The dog came out of his house in time to take a bite out of my partner's rear.

The dog came out of his house in time to take a bite out of my partner's rear.

The yard lights came on, and I discovered my partner in a lot of pain. He was walking around in circles. A large German shepherd chained to a dog house had bitten him. The dog had a current rabies shot. I got the dog owner's name and address for our report and we left for the hospital.

He had a good bite on his left buttock—four large puncture wounds and the area was black and blue. His pants and underwear were torn. They washed out the wound and gave him a tetanus shot and some pain pills. The doctor told him to check for infection and if he sees any to get to the doctor fast. He said the blue dye in the new police pants could cause a worse infection than the bite could. They taped gauze over the bite. We went to the central police station where we made out more reports.

He took the rest of the night off, but he was there for roll call the next day. I joked with him and said, “Aren’t you glad your mother always told you to wear clean underwear when you went somewhere because you never know when a dog might bite your butt and you will have to go to the hospital?”

Everyone had a chuckle. The city replaced his pants.

I recall one unusual barking dog call I received. It was around 10:30 on a hot sticky night. I parked in front of the house and shut the engine off and sat there for a few minutes and listened for a dog barking, but I didn’t hear one. When I knocked on the door, some dogs barked but it was more of a yap. The porch light came on and I heard a man trying to hush them. An elderly man opened the door.

I told him I had a complaint about his dogs barking. He said the dogs were his wife’s, and she had them for medical reasons. I asked what her medical problems were. He said she had heart and pulmonary problems and allergies. He said they were Mexican Chihuahuas and something about them helped her breathe. He asked if I would like to see the dogs and I said yes.

He opened the door behind him and out came the dogs—lots of them. I asked him how many of them they had. He said he wasn’t sure but thought there were twenty-three. A woman in the next room called out, “Harold, who are you talking to?”

Harold said, “I’m talking to a police officer. He is here about the dogs barking.”

She said, "Have him come in here." She was a large woman, perhaps 260 pounds.

She was lying in a hospital bed, which was raised up so she could watch a television set that was hung on the wall by her feet. She was on oxygen and there were several of these dogs in bed with her. Someone had built a ramp so the dogs could get in and out of her bed by themselves with someone picking them up or putting them down.

I told her someone complained about the dogs barking at night. She said they did bark when they heard a noise. I noticed the window was raised, but it was still hot in the room. I suggested they purchase a window unit air conditioner. She and her dogs would be cooler and they would not hear noise at night so they wouldn't be barking. With the house shut up and the air conditioner running the neighbors wouldn't hear her dogs if they did bark.

I suggested she check with her doctor and find out the best number of dogs she should have to control her breathing problem. I was surprised that the house didn't smell with so many dogs in it, but they had litter boxes in one room and the old man kept them clean. I told them they would have to have a kennel license to keep all of the dogs they had.

I don't know what they did about their dogs. I drove past their house about a week later and noticed a large air conditioner sticking out of her bedroom window. I never received any more radio calls there so the dogs must have stopped their barking or the neighbors couldn't hear them over the air conditioner when it was running.

One afternoon I was taking a stolen bike report at a house. The woman had the bill of sale and the registration.

I was sitting at her kitchen table making the report when I thought I saw something run across the floor.

She said, “Did you see something?”

I said, “I think I did but whatever it was it was sure fast.”

She said it was a jerboa—a small nocturnal leaping rodent from North Africa with very long back legs. They bought some of them for their children and they got loose in their basement and now they were all over the house. I told her my one son said he wanted one of them, but after that I didn’t think he would be getting one.

A man called the police one fall morning. He said he was awakened by a noise in his driveway next to his house. He looked out of his window and saw a tow truck parked behind his brand new 1967 Rambler in his driveway. The hood on his car was raised, and a man was busy doing something under the hood.

He got dressed and went outside and asked the man what he was doing. The man was real nice. The auto dealership sent him out to check the anti-freeze in the car’s radiator to make sure it wouldn’t freeze because they didn’t have a record of it being checked.

He asked, “They didn’t call you, did they?”

No, they hadn’t called.

“I’m so sorry. I hope I didn’t wake you up,” and then suggested the car’s owner call the dealership and ask for the garage foreman and tell him you’re upset. There was no reason for this to have happened.

He went in to call the dealership and heard the tow truck start up. He talked to the garage foreman who told

The truck was gone and so was his radiator.

him they hadn't sent anyone out to check his anti-freeze.

He hung up and ran outside. The truck was gone and so was his radiator. Only four bolts and two radiator hose clamps had held it in the car. The anti-freeze made a mess in his driveway.

The man didn't remember anything about the tow truck. It was either a light yellow or green color. The suspect was a white male, 5 feet 10 inches tall, 200 pounds, forty-five to fifty years old, wearing blue coveralls. He wasn't sure if he would be able to recognize him if he saw him again.

I finished filling out the report and told the man if he could think of anything else to call it in to the detective bureau. I went to my cruiser and hit back in service I thought to myself *so much for eyewitnesses.*

I received a call to meet the detectives at an address I recognized because I knew some people who had lived there at one time. The detective was waiting in his car when I arrived. He said the parents of a well-known burglar lived there and he had a search warrant for the bedroom where the burglar stayed. I told the detective we better have some more people here if the burglar and his father are in there because they are bad news.

He said the burglar was in jail and we could handle the old man. He wanted a police uniformed officer there when he knocked on the door. I said, "Let's go."

The detective showed them the search warrant and told them he would give them a copy when we left and a receipt for anything we might take.

They didn't give us any problem. We went into the bedroom and he told the parents they would have to stay out of the room while we searched it. He closed the door and that's when we discovered twenty to thirty keys hung on a piece of plywood attached to the back of the door. Each key had a tag tied on it identifying which door lock it fit on different businesses in the city.

He said, "This is the key I'm looking for." It was to a safety deposit box at one of our local banks.

He checked out the whole room looking for the second safety deposit box key or other ones. He wrote down the serial numbers on all of the items that had one if they were in plain view, and we took the key board. I asked him if he would let me know if the safety deposit box key was the one they wanted.

That afternoon I got a call to phone the detective bureau. It was my friend with the search warrant. Six months earlier one of the officers had his portable radio stolen out of his cruiser. That day, when they opened the safety deposit box, the only thing in it was the stolen police portable radio. Records showed he was sole owner of the box and he was the only one who had signed in or out to use it. They had him dead to rights on this one.

They were going to file a bitch on him (habitual criminal) this time, and he would be gone for a long time. He was killed in a fight before his trial date came up so he was never tried, but this was the last rap he would ever beat.

Randal, being a good host, grabbed up his sawed-off shotgun.

I had an unusual shooting call on a Friday night. I know it was a Friday night because the packing houses paid every Friday, and this group got together to drink beer and play poker at Randal's house on payday night. Everyone was having a good time until they caught someone cheating.

Randal, being a good host, grabbed up his sawed-off shotgun. The cheater turned to run and Randal shot him in the back of his head. It was the man's lucky day. It was a real old shell and the lead bird shot didn't penetrate his skull, but it peppered his head.

The doctors left most of the shot in his scalp since there was no way they could remove all of it. We turned Randal over to the detective bureau.

Every officer had a notepad in his car where we recorded everything we did each day and the time we did it. At the end of the day we would use it to make out our Daily Activity Report. Once the report was made, the pages went into the trash. I wish I had saved mine.

While I was still working as a regional investigator out of the detective bureau in the fall of 1975, I received a radio call to meet the cruiser officers with an attempted suicide at the University Hospital. The victim was a twenty-four-year-old white female who looked identical to Elizabeth Taylor, the movie star. This was the second time she had tried to end her life. The first time was six months prior to this one when she drank a bottle of Lysol disinfectant.

She was married and they had two children. She also had a lot of mental problems. I had investigated her first attempt at suicide. She was under the care of a psychiatrist then for depression. This time she drank a bottle of drain cleaner, and the prognosis didn't look good.

She wasn't pretty anymore. The drain cleaner had destroyed her face from her nose down. It was nothing but a chunk of raw meat with white teeth sticking out of it. The skin was eaten off by the caustic drain cleaner. It had to be so painful for her before she lost consciousness.

I cannot begin to imagine the damage done to her internal organs as the drain cleaner ate through them and the pain she must have endured.

I talked to her husband. He said she was doing fine as long as she stayed on her medication, but he thought she must have quit taking it. She had to have just bought the drain cleaner because he said he got rid of everything they had in the house after she drank the Lysol. He checked the house the night before, and there was no drain cleaner in the house then.

The doctor finally came out of the Emergency Room and asked for the husband. He told him he was sorry they had done everything they could for her, but they couldn't save her. I phoned the county coroner and advised him.

In the early part of the winter of 1966 we received a call about two fishermen falling through the ice on the east side of Carter Lake by the fire station at Eppley Airfield. When we arrived, the firefighters were ready to leave the scene. The fishermen had been able to get back on the ice by themselves and they got in their car and left. They were two lucky people.

We had a man on the west side of the lake who wasn't so lucky. It was in the spring of 1968 and the ice was gone, but the water was still ice cold. This man had built his own paddle boat. It looked like a professional job. He should not have been on the lake because the water was too cold and he didn't have a life jacket on. I can understand his wanting to try out his new invention, but something went wrong and it tipped over, throwing him into the cold water.

The lake had just turned over and the water was real cloudy and dirty, but the rescue people were able find the body with their poles and recover it. What was meant to be a festive occasion quickly turned out to be a tragedy. This was one of the calls I tried to forget—and thought I had.

Here's another one I would rather forget. It was a hot summer afternoon in 1962. I received a call to make an investigation at a Mom and Pop grocery store on South Twentieth Street. I went into the store and asked if someone had called. The owner of the store said he called.

They had an apartment over the store, which they rented out to an older single man who lived there by himself. They hadn't seen him for a while. They tried to call him but no one answered the phone. He wanted someone to go with him into the man's apartment to see if everything was okay. I said, "Let's go."

We went out the front door of the store to a second door also located on the front of the building. He used his key to unlock the door to a stairway to the second floor.

Once you have smelled one, you never forget it.

He asked, "What's that?" pointing to a clear fluid with brown specks in it that had run down the steps and was now on the landing.

I didn't know. Then I smelled the stench of a decomposing human body. Once you have smelled one, you never forget it. I told him, "Don't get any of that stuff on your shoes."

"What is it?"

I said, "I think it's fluid out of a decomposing body."

We went upstairs and on our left side of a hallway was a door. The fluid trail came from under this door. I told the man that what we were going to find wasn't going to be very pleasant. The smell was really bad now.

He unlocked the door and opened it. He gagged and ran down the stairs. I could hear him regurgitating outside. I had a couple of involuntary spasms in my stomach but fortunately I didn't vomit.

About four feet inside of the doorway on the floor was the bloated body of a dead man. His legs had split like a weenie does when you hold it too close to the fire while roasting it to make a hot dog. This is where the fluid came from that ran down the steps. He was on his stomach but he was bloated so badly his hips and buttocks were raised up in the air about three feet off the floor.

The green flies had gotten to him, and the maggots were having a feast. His head was turned so I could see that his mouth, nose, and where his eyes had been were full of maggots. I was getting used to the smell now.

I knew if I left the room I would get sick when I tried to come back into it so I stayed there. I used the deceased man's telephone to call the detective bureau and the county coroner. Since nothing in the house was disturbed and the doors had to be locked with a key, the detective bureau didn't suspect foul play and said to make the report and turn it in.

The coroner came out and took the dead man's billfold out of his back pocket, and we counted his money. He had me list it on the report that he took the billfold and the money. He had the body taken to the county morgue for an autopsy. They put the body in a body bag and covered it with a white powder before they zipped the bag closed.

The pathologist was able to tell he had died from a massive heart attack. I was able to get home from work before my wife did and put my uniform in the clothes dryer with one of those blue paper things. I set it on air fluff and let it run for thirty minutes while I took a shower. It worked; the smell was gone. I put the uniform in my car trunk and took it to the cleaners the next day.

- Twenty -

TOWING THE LINE

I was assigned to work in the police tow lot in July of 1987. I knew little about how the tow lot operated but was willing to learn. I discovered they had a few problems but nothing that couldn't be corrected. They were having one auto auction a month, and the lot would be full again in two weeks. Then they would only accept cars at the lot from accidents. Attendants had very little to do during the next two weeks before the next auction would clear the lot.

Two civilian inspectors worked on the street towing vehicles for different violations. Once the lot was full, they couldn't tow any cars, so they also had little to do. There was a backlog of cars waiting to be towed but no place to put them.

One of the men who worked in the tow lot scheduled his own days off, and one woman who worked in the office set her own hours as to when she would come to work and when she would go home. She was the person responsible for getting the new titles for the cars so they could be sold at the auction. When she took a day off, no one knew how to do her job. So the backlog increased even more.

At that time any car on the lot not claimed after ten days could be sold. But she was waiting thirty days before she applied for the title. The cars were sitting in the lot twenty days longer than the law required.

I had a meeting with my supervisor and told him what factors I felt were impeding the operation of the tow lot and what could be done to correct it. He got back to me and said, "Correct the problems."

The first thing I did was to put the two people who were on their own flex times back on regular hours and days off like their coworkers. Of course, they were not happy. Grievances were filed but they were unfounded. I started cross training on all the office jobs.

One woman quit and the one who had filed a grievance before complained again. We increased the number of auctions we had from once a month to twice a month. We now applied for new titles after ten days like the law said. One man who worked in the tow lot transferred out. We replaced the two people who left, and with the increase in auctions we now had room in the lot. There was no excuse for our inspectors not to be towing cars in. Their backlog was getting smaller.

The uniformed officers were once again towing in vehicles that were found to be in violation in their districts. I could see it was only a matter of time before the lot would be full again. Even with all the changes, we needed a larger lot.

The trailer was full of rats.

One of our inspectors towed in three vehicles and a trailer loaded with junk from a private lot. They didn't realize the trailer was full of rats until they were towing it down the street to the impound lot and saw the rats jumping out of the trailer and bounding down the street in their rear view mirrors.

The driver told us about the rats, so I had him park the trailer at the far end of the lot. I called the exterminator who set out some poison grain for them in boxes and said we should unload the trailer and haul everything to the dump. I called public works and told them what we had. They came out the next day and hauled everything away. The rats were gone.

A few days later we had a mouse in the office. One person screamed and climbed up on her desk and carried on. We had a lunch room, and I had told everyone before they were to eat their lunch in there and that no food was to be kept in their desks. They were told to keep it in the refrigerator in the lunch room so we wouldn't get any mice in the office.

I had a feeling another complaint would soon be coming, so I called the exterminator right then. He came out the next morning and put poison out for the mice. He noticed some cookies on a desk and told the woman if she didn't leave food out for the mice they wouldn't come in.

I received a copy of the complaint she made that afternoon. She said there was a mouse in the office, and I laughed and didn't do anything about it. My reply to her complaint was this, "I don't think I laughed but it isn't often when one sees a 300-pound woman standing on a desk screaming at a 4-ounce mouse on the floor."

I reminded her that I had phoned the exterminator as soon as I knew there was a mouse in the office. I told her many times before not to have food at her desk because it drew the mice into the office but she had ignored me. She had an open package of cookies on her desk when the exterminator came and he told her about it. I never heard anything more about the complaint.

I heard the local auto auction was going to be moving out of the city to a larger location, and they were going to be putting their present property on the market. We were outgrowing our present location at Twenty-fourth and Hickory and we needed to be more centrally located in the city. The auto auction location near Seventy-eighth and F streets would be perfect for us. It was larger than we needed, but we could sell off the buildings and part of the land and recoup a good part of our cost. I talked to my supervisor about it and he thought it was a good idea. He said he would look into it.

A few months later he called and said they bought half of the land from the auto auction people. He wanted me to meet with an architect to draw up plans for a new office building for the police impound lot. We went with a steel building with a stone front. I wanted a heated area where we could park our equipment, and I wanted it large enough so the crime lab could process a semi-tractor inside it if they needed to. I wanted a larger storage area for the other property we sold at our auctions. I thought big because I knew some of the people above the police level would have to have their input and changes would be made.

We lost some and we gained some, but the building was approved and under construction. The impound lot was now making money, and the employees were finally going to have a nice place to work. Most of the employees were new and the complaints had almost stopped. One of the inspectors was padding his daily report to make it look like he was doing more work than he actually was. He put down that he talked to several people and gave them ten-day notices to correct their violations when he hadn't. I wrote him up and sent the paperwork to my supervisor.

The street inspector I wrote up apparently had some political influence because I received a visit from a political appointee in City Hall who wanted to know why I was checking on this employee and why I wrote him up. And he wanted my response in writing in his office that same day.

I asked if he wanted me to hand carry it or send it through the chain of command. I could tell this upset him, but he said to bring it to him. I said, "Fine, but you should know I'm going to send a copy to my Union representative, and a second copy will be sent through the chain of command."

He didn't say a thing; he just stormed out of my office.

I called my supervisor and told him about my visitor. He took me to see the chief. The chief wasn't happy about this man coming down to the tow lot without going through the chain of command first. The chief advised me not to send anything to him.

The personnel rules state one must follow an order even if they think it is wrong. Then they should file a grievance, so I delivered the following note to his office, "Here is the information you requested when you came down to the tow lot this morning. You asked why I was checking on [John Doe] and why I wrote him up. I checked on the party because I am his supervisor and that is my job. I wrote him up because he made false reports. All of the evidence has been sent to my supervisor."

I noted on the report to him that copies were sent to my Union representative and through the chain of command to insure he would receive my report. He was not in his office when I delivered the note. I never heard any more about it.

I don't know if any action was taken on the street inspector because he seldom came into the office when I was there. I think he got the word to cool it.

One afternoon I was busy in my office at the impound lot with some paperwork when I noticed a shiny black, low-ride Lincoln Town Car with blacked out windows and 22-inch dubs (wheels) turn into the parking area. They parked away from the other cars. Five people got out of the car: one black man and four white women. They must have been on their way to a costume party because he was dressed like a pimp and the women were dressed like prostitutes.

He was dressed like a pimp and the women were dressed like prostitutes.

The reason for their visit was to get the man's "ride" released from the impound lot. The man wasn't happy when he found out what he had to pay to get his car back, and he was starting to get loud. I went out to the desk and asked him if there was a problem. He said he didn't think he should have to pay what the clerk wanted. I told him he could pay it under protest and go to court and he might get some of it back.

He wanted to know what he had to do to protest it. I gave him a copy of the form to fill out. He looked at it and said he was going to pay the charges. He couldn't take time off to go to court because it would cost him more to do that than what he would save if they gave him all of his money back. He paid his money and went with the attendant to get his car. Three of the women went out and got into the Lincoln. The fourth one stayed inside at the counter.

She handed me her business card and said she owned a massage parlor and wanted to know if I had ever had a massage. I told her I hadn't but I had thought about it and I might get one someday. She said to give her a call and she would set up an appointment. She said she would give me a full body massage, and it would be complimentary. I thanked her and said I would think about it.

Her card showed her business was located in a house in a rough area of town. After she left, my crew gave me a hard time about what she had said. I told them they had dirty minds. She was just trying to build up her massage business whenever she thought she might be able to. I said I was going to call her for an appointment and went into my office.

I phoned a friend on the vice squad and told him about my new friend and gave him the information I had on her. My crew didn't know who I had called, but they never said anymore about the young lady. I have had a couple of massages since then, but I still don't know what a full body massage includes and I'm not going to ask.

After every auto auction I would deposit the money at the city cashier's office and got to know the people who worked there. One time when I went to make a deposit, it was the birthday of the woman who always waited on me. I asked her if she was going to have a birthday cake. She said she had never had a birthday cake in her life. When she was growing up, her family never had cakes and now that she is grown she never bakes one for herself.

I went down to the bakery and bought one cupcake and asked them to put it in a box. I always picked up donuts there for the tow lot people on auction day so they knew me. He asked why I wanted the cupcake in a box and I told him the story.

He asked if I wanted a candle on it. Not only that, he wrote Happy Birthday on it. It was real neat. I picked up a birthday card on my way back to the cashier's office.

When I stepped back inside the cashier's office, she said, "What did you forget?"

"This," and gave her the box with the card on top of it.

She didn't know what to say.

"Look at the card and open the box," I said.

When she saw the cake, tears came in her eyes and I said Happy Birthday and left.

When I saw her the next time, I asked how the cake was. She said she never ate it but took it home and showed it to her husband, then she put it away. She said it was the first birthday cake she ever had and she was going to save it and the card. She thanked me again. I felt good that I made her birthday one that she would remember. She always gave me super service.

I believe you reap what you sow. And it has worked for me.

Police work wasn't always all about catching bad guys. We had plenty of opportunities to be goodwill ambassadors in the community.

One summer during the late 1960s when we were having racial problems, I volunteered to be a camp counselor at a summer camp sponsored by the city, the public schools, the YMCA, and other organizations. All of the counselors were either police officers or school teachers. The Y provided the campground, cabins, sheets, blankets, horses, canoes, fishing equipment, and other supplies.

The campers, underprivileged kids, came from the housing project in the area of the city they called the Ghetto and later called Little Vietnam. The camp was located eighty miles away from the city out in the country next to a river in a wooded area.

We chartered a bus to take forty boys and five adults out to the camp. We stopped for lunch on our way out, but we made arrangements ahead of time at the restaurant so they were waiting for us. A lot of people did stare at us. We finished eating before the lunch crowd came in, and we were on our way again.

The campground had about twenty cabins, a mess hall, a boat house, a stable, a fish house, a swimming lake, and a bath house. Each cabin had three old Army bunk beds, six lockers, and one table and chair in it. That meant there would be five campers and one counselor to a cabin.

I had a packet with the names of the kids assigned to my cabin and our schedules were in it. When we got off the bus at the campground, I called out their names and told them mine and what our cabin number was.

I said, "Let's see if we can find it."

Our cabin (number 18) was close to the bath house, which was nice if you had to make a late night run. I showed them a list of the things we were expected to do, and one with the different times we were scheduled to go horseback riding, swimming, canoeing, and fishing. One thing to do was to make the beds and sweep the cabin floor.

"If we work together," I told them, "this won't be so bad. There are five of you and we have five days of making beds and sweeping the floor. That means you only have to sweep one time, and I'll help you. I was in the Air Force for four years, and I can make a mean bed. I know you can too. I will show you how and then we can go to breakfast. Maybe you can teach an old dog like me some new tricks."

I reminded them not to be afraid to ask me if there was something they did not understand.

These kids were eleven years old, but they had to grow up in a hurry, and they were street smart. They were sizing me up most of the time. After breakfast we went to the stables to ride the horses.

There were five horses for the six of us to ride, which meant one of us would not be riding. I said I really didn't care if I ever rode a horse again. If it was okay with them I would skip riding the horses. I said I would meet them at the swimming hole when they got back.

The water was chilly but lying on the sand beach was nice. The troops came back, and they had to tell me about their horseback riding adventure and how they saw a deer in the trees. We swam and played on the beach until lunch time.

After lunch we went canoeing. Of course, everyone wore a life jacket. None of them had ever been in a canoe before, so it was interesting to watch them try to navigate the thing. Before the week was over they looked like they had been canoeing forever. We fished every evening in the river and caught some nice fish. We had a fish fry on Friday, and everyone seemed to have a good time. We in cabin 18 became friends.

Some of them asked if I was a cop or a teacher. I told them I would let them know at breakfast on the morning we left to go home. The week had gone by so fast. At breakfast one of them asked when I was going to tell if I was a cop or a teacher.

I asked them what they thought I was. They said a teacher.

"Sorry. I'm a cop," I said.

"You can't be," they said.

"Why not?"

It was quiet until one of the boys said, "Because your legs are too skinny," and everyone laughed.

I think that quiet moment said a lot. They never had a summer camp after that year. It was a success but I believe it was too costly.

One of my instructors brought me some literature on a pilot program the Boy Scouts were about to start in the housing projects in our city. It was a joint venture with public housing and the police department. They were asking for police officers to become scout leaders. The city would pay regular wages while you held your meetings. This officer wanted to know if I would be interested in starting a troop with him in a certain housing project. I said I would if he would be the scout master and I was his assistant.

The housing project provided space for our meetings and sent out flyers announcing when our first meeting was to be held. Man, did we have a crowd. Every mother in the project who had a son dropped him off and drove away. When the meeting was over, the mothers never came back for them.

The housing project manager finally told them to go home and they left. I don't know why we didn't think of that. We handed out applications to all of the boys at the meeting and told them to fill them out and bring them back to the next meeting. Only a handful came back for the next meeting.

We tried to hold regular meetings but most of the boys were not interested in scouting. They liked the sacks we provided and the field trips. We reached a few of them but no parent ever showed up or became involved. The troop got smaller and smaller with each meeting. There weren't enough boys living in the projects who were interested in scouting.

The troop was destined to fail before it started. It was disbanded in less than a year for lack of interest. There was only so much one could do. I guess it was better that we tried and failed than not to have tried at all. None of the scout troops in any of the housing projects survived their first year.

If we weren't trying to help the youth, we were often called on to take care of the elderly.

We received a disturbance call at a service station one night around 9:30 p.m. When we arrived there, an elderly man wearing an expensive brown pinstriped suit was yelling at the attendant. He wanted to know who gave him permission to build a gas station there, and what did they do with his house. We thought he might be suffering from dementia.

An elderly man wearing an expensive brown pinstriped suit was yelling at the attendant.

We checked with radio to see if any nursing homes had reported a missing person. One nursing home ten miles away from where we were had reported a man missing at 5:00 p.m. when he failed to come down to the dining room for supper. Radio gave us his name and description. He fit the description so I asked him his name and he told us. He was the missing person.

It is hard to believe a ninety-two-year-old man could get ten miles away from where he was last seen without any money. Radio told us to take him to his son's house, which was only three miles away from where we were. His son was a medical doctor. He asked where we found his dad. When we told him, he said that is where his father's farm was over fifty years before. He had sold it and moved in town. The old man knew who his son was and he was happy to see him.

The doctor/son said, "I wonder if they will ever find a cure for dementia. Look at him. He's ninety-two, and I'd bet he walked the ten miles down to his farm from the nursing home, but right now he doesn't know where the nursing home is. It won't be long and he won't know who I am."

He paused for a second and said, "I want to thank you for bringing him home. I'll take him back to the home and find out how he escaped. It should be interesting to find out what they have to say."

One evening, I received a radio call to see the owner of a local restaurant about the well-being of an elderly customer of his. He said for the past seven years they have been delivering a dinner meal to this elderly woman at her home. They have a key to her front door so they ring her doorbell and set the tray of food with dishes and silverware on the floor just inside of the door, and they close and lock the door. They pick up the tray about an hour later.

He said they seldom see her, and they send a bill to her guardian once a month for her food. He said, "She is a hoarder. Newspapers are stacked throughout the house from floor to ceiling. There are only small pathways going through it."

He said when his delivery person stopped to pick up the tray, her food had not been touched. It was still on the floor where he had left it. He said he was afraid something was wrong with her and wanted someone with authority to go with him to check on her.

We drove over in my cruiser. Her house was one of those huge old two-story homes built in the early 1900s. We rang the doorbell several times, and no one answered, so he used his key and we went inside.

She was sitting at a table eating her cold supper.

It was even worse than he had described. The food tray was gone. It was dark now and there was only one small light bulb hanging down on a wire from the ceiling in the center of the room. We could hardly squeeze through the small pathway between the stacks of papers.

We went through the first room into a second one. The only way we could tell we were in a different room was because the light bulb hanging from the ceiling was not as bright as the one in the first room. I was glad I brought my flashlight so we could see where we were going.

As we went into a third room, I saw the woman. She was sitting at a table eating her cold supper—her back to us—watching a rerun of Milton Berle in the Texaco Star Theater on a small TV set on the table.

The owner of the restaurant called her name and she turned to look at us. Her skin and hair were snow white—as if she hadn't been outside in years. She needed to get out of the house and into the sunlight. I understood why she stayed in the house. Her neighborhood wasn't the most desirable place to live as it once was.

She had to be in her nineties and could not have weighed a hundred pounds. She didn't seem startled because we were there. He told her we came to check on her when the delivery man noticed she had not eaten her meal when he came to pick up her tray. We wanted to make sure she was all right. She smiled and thanked us for coming.

She said she had lost track of time and was late eating supper. He told her we wouldn't bother her any longer and they would pick up the tray when they bring her food tomorrow. She said that would be fine. We locked up the door when we left. On the way back to the restaurant he said he was glad she was okay but he knew some day it wasn't going to be that way.

He said a lawyer was getting paid good money to look after her well-being, but it didn't look like he was doing a very good job of it. She had no family left, so she sat in that dark house day after day, watching her little TV set, never seeing anyone, and being scared to death that someone was going to break in and hurt her. She was afraid to go outside for the same reason. She sat and waited for the grim reaper to call her name.

The restaurant owner felt there was a better way to care for her. I suggested the lawyer might need a little nudging. He agreed.

I later heard the woman moved into a nursing home and her house was sold. She finally was around people and had someone to talk to. Perhaps she even went outside and sat in the sunshine and watched the birds or looked at the flowers. She didn't have to be afraid anymore, thanks to the concern of a restaurant owner and the day she was late eating her supper.

In a similar incident, I received a call to meet the rescue squad with a sick party. It turned out to be man in his nineties who was suffering from malnutrition. He was literally starving to death. It so happened his guardian was a court-appointed attorney.

A neighbor of the old man said she looked in on him about once a week and found him hungry and without food. She fed him and called the lawyer and left a message for him to call her. She waited three hours for the lawyer to call before she called the rescue squad.

I called for the crime lab to come for pictures. While they were there, the attorney showed up with a small sack of groceries.

I said, "You're a little late with them."

"What do you mean?"

I showed him the empty fridge, the empty pantry, the empty waste basket, and then I took him outside and showed him the empty garbage can. I said they picked it up five days ago.

I said, "I have pictures of everything I showed you, and they show there has not been any food in this house for at least five days. The pictures they get at the hospital of the old man and the doctor's report will show it has been a lot longer."

He didn't say a word.

I went on, "Several of the neighbors are talking with the news media right now. You are being paid to look out for this man and you're not doing it. It takes a real sick person to starve someone. I don't know if the courts know what you're doing but they will. I'm sure someone will be contacting you real soon."

I don't know if the courts did anything with him. I do know the old man was never neglected by anyone again. The neighbors made sure of it.

My partner and I made a disturbance call to a particular apartment building on the average of three times a month. This fifty-seven-year-old man, who was a graduate engineer and the owner of the apartment building, would go to the club on Friday night after work and have too much to drink.

> Her toenails were about three and a half inches long and they twisted and curled down under her feet.

He would come home to his invalid mother who lived with him and start yelling at her because all of his shortcomings were her fault. If he had not had to care for her, he would have married and had children, he blamed her. It was her fault he didn't have his own family and he went on and on never stopping. He brow beat her unbearably but never laid a hand her. He didn't have to.

The old woman was always in her pajamas wearing a robe when we were there, and she never got out of the recliner she was lying in. I don't know if she could walk. Her toenails were about three and a half inches long and they twisted and curled down under her feet. There was no way she could wear slippers or shoes over them if she wanted to. Her neglected fingernails were just as long. Her white hair was long and full of dread locks and looked as if it had never been brushed.

All the woman wanted was for him to shut up and go to bed. She wanted to be left alone, she said. She didn't know how much more of his abuse she could take.

I told the son, "Look at her. She is your mother. Why don't you have someone cut her nails and fix her hair?"

"That's none of your business," he fired back.

I told him if he didn't shut his mouth and go to bed and stay there, I would make it my business. He went to his room and he must have stayed there as we never got a call back from her that night.

Two weeks later we had a disturbance call there again and we sent him to bed. He never had her nails cut. I didn't understand why. He had the money to have it done. The following Wednesday we got a call to make an investigation call at their apartment. He had come home from work and found his mother dead. She was lying on her recliner.

The son was crying and carrying on like you wouldn't believe. Perhaps he was feeling a little guilty over the way he had treated her over the years. I contacted the acting county coroner and gave him the information on the deceased. Since she died at home without an attending physician, there would have to be an autopsy to determine the cause of death. The coroner sent someone to pick up her body. He wanted to talk with her son.

We finished our report and waited with the man until they picked up his mother's body. He didn't say much and neither did we. They took the body away and we left. She didn't have to take any more of his abuse.

We received a disturbance call where an elderly woman cut down her neighbor's tree, which fell across his driveway blocking his car so he couldn't get out to go to work. I went over to talk to the woman.

She was in her eighties and said she was trimming the branches that hung over on her property when the tree fell over. I told her she couldn't cut down a tree when it wasn't on her property. The tree was about twenty-five-feet tall with an eighteen-inch diameter.

I told the man about the only thing he could do now was to get someone to take him to work or call a cab. The next day he could hire a tree person to saw it up and haul it away. Then he would have to sue her to get his money back.

I gave him my card and said I'd be a witness for him, but I didn't know how he would ever collect from her.

A tree trimmer friend of mine was driving by and stopped. I shook my head and told him the story and he laughed. He told his helper to get the twenty-inch chain saw out of the truck. He said, "We'll take care of this."

They sawed two-foot sections out of the tree clearing an area wide enough for the man to get his car out. The man asked what he owed him, and my friend said, "This one is on the house."

I don't know how the old lady managed to saw on the tree enough that it split and fell down. She was using an old hand saw. The neighbor living across from them came home and walked over to see what was going on. When he learned what she had done, he said he would get the neighbors together and they would clean it up. The neighbors also said they were going to talk with her and let her know they would help her with the tree trimming in the future if she would just ask.

I drove by a few days later. The area was cleaned up. They even sawed the stump off at ground level. I never had another call there, so I figured she must have been getting along with her neighbor now.

"I hope we get there before your water breaks."

The old woman still mowed her grass every week, carried her garbage out to the curb, and grew a small garden each year. She drove her car to the grocery store, to the doctor, and to church. She was still sharp and always walked fast wherever she went and she held her head up high. She was a proud person.

You often hear about police delivering babies. Here's my story. My partner was just out of recruit training, and we were transporting a pregnant woman to the hospital. Her labor pains were real close together. I said, "I hope we get there before your water breaks."

"It broke before I called," she said.

We had less than a mile to go before we got to the hospital, but I told my partner to turn on the red light and siren and to expedite. The woman was in real pain now and was screaming so loudly we almost didn't need a siren.

A doctor and two nurses met us at the door. The doctor got right in the back seat with her, he told the nurse to get the cart out there now because she was starting to crown. They just got inside the hallway of the hospital when the baby was born, so they went right into the emergency room and shut the door. We returned to our car. We never found out if it was a boy or girl.

My partner asked me what I meant when I said I hope we make it to the hospital before your water breaks. I explained everything to him. Then he wanted to know what the doctor meant when he said she's starting to crown. I explained that to him too, and after our father and son talk we went to eat our dinner. I never wanted to get that close to delivering a baby again.

My partner was rather naïve on some subjects but he wasn't afraid to ask questions. He was a quick study so I knew he'd be okay.

Sometimes people take the law into their own hands. Like this incident. When I was a regional investigator, I received a call to meet a cruiser officer with a shooting at the baseball field in one of our city parks. When I arrived, two uniformed officers were talking to a well-dressed elderly black man. He was holding his left hand with his right hand and his little finger on his left hand was about torn off.

The man told me two girls softball teams were playing there. The home team was black, and the visiting team was white. He stated the man he shot was drinking beer and yelling bad stuff at the white girls who were about twelve years old.

I asked him what the bad stuff was.

The old man said he called the girls honky bitches, hoes, and yelled about what he would like them to do for him.

They stopped the game and were loading up their equipment to leave. He walked over to the man to talk with him, but the man was too drunk to listen so the old man walked back to where he had been sitting. The drunk man followed him and picked up a three-foot-long piece of a two-by-four that had been torn from the bleachers. He told the old man he should mind his own business and swung the board at him. The elderly man raised his hand to ward off the blow and received the injury to his hand.

They thought the drunk was going to kill the old guy until he pulled out his gun and shot the loud drunk.

The drunk drew the board back and was going to hit him a second time. The old man said that's when he pulled out his piece and fired once hitting the man in his chest. Two women who witnessed the shooting said that's what happened. They thought the drunk was going to kill the old guy until he pulled out his gun and shot the loud drunk.

The uniformed officers gave me their report. I noticed the old man was eighty-four years old. I said I would take him to the hospital to have his hand taken care of and check on the party who was shot. I learned the drunk was DOA at the hospital. I checked to see if the gun was registered and it was.

The old man had a dislocated finger and two lacerations that required stitches. When the doctors were finished working on him, we went to the police station for booking. I was going to call the county attorney who was on duty to see if some kind of bond could be set so he wouldn't have to sit in jail over the weekend until he could go to court on Monday morning. He was on heart medicine and blood thinners.

I lucked out. The attorney was there at the jail. I laid out everything for him and he asked, "What do you think you have?"

I said, "Nothing. It was self-defense."

He said, "Give him his gun and take him home."

On our way to the old man's house I asked if he would like to stop for burger and a soda. He said he would like that. We ate our supper and sat there for a while and talked.

When I dropped him off, he said thank you and shut the door. I slept well that night.

I remember one bitter cold winter afternoon when I was driving out the river road. We had had a blizzard the night before, and the road was still only one lane in many places. I came upon a car that was stopped facing me on the other side of the road. I saw it had a flat rear tire on the driver's side of the car. There was a black man and two small children in the car.

I didn't want to block the road by stopping there, so I continued going down the road for about a half mile where I was able to turn around. I went back to the car and stopped behind it. I turned on my red lights and stepped out of the cruiser. The driver got out of his car at the same time. I said, "It looks like you have a problem."

He said, "I do I have a flat tire and my spare is flat too. I've been sitting here for two hours and no one has stopped. I have my two babies in the car. I was afraid to try and carry them all the way into town in this cold, and I don't dare leave them in the car by themselves. I'm about out of gas. I have been running the car for a while to keep it warm. Then cut it off to save gas."

I said, "Put your babies in my car." He took one and I took the other. They were cold. We put them in the back seat, and I turned the heater on high. I told radio I would be out of service assisting a motorist.

I told him to put the flat tire in the front seat with me and he could ride in the back with his children. We drove two miles before we found a service station. They put air in the tire and put it in a tank of water to find the leak. There was no leak. Someone must have let the air out of it.

The service station attendant said there was no charge for what he did. I told the motorist after he puts the spare tire on the car, I'll follow him back to the gas station so he can have his flat tire fixed and buy some gas before he runs out.

"The kids can ride with me in the warm car," I told him.

He said, "You are the last person I ever thought would help me. When you first went by, I never expected you to come back."

"You are the last person I ever thought would help me."

"You may have a good reason for feeling the way you do," I said, "but just because there is one bad apple in a basket doesn't mean all of the apples in the basket are bad."

He didn't say much after that. When he finished putting the spare on his car, he said, "I want to thank you for all you have done for me today."

"No problem," I replied.

"And I'll remember what you said," he told me.

Sometimes the Good Samaritans come to the aid of police. I was driving to work one day when I had a flat tire. I pulled over to the curb and stopped. The rear tire on the driver's side was flat. I opened the trunk lid to get my spare tire and jack when a car stopped behind me. I was in uniform at the time.

A man dressed in a suit got out of the back seat of the car and walked up to me and said, "It looks like you have a problem."

"I must have run over a nail but it won't take long to put the spare tire on," I said.

It was a real hot sticky day. He said, "You will get your uniform dirty and all sweaty. I'll have Rodney do it for you." He motioned for the driver to come to him.

Rodney got out of the car. He was wearing a uniform and must have been this man's chauffeur. I looked at his Cadillac limousine with a glass divider between the driver and the passenger area. I told Rodney he didn't have to change my tire for me and he said, "Yes, I do."

I couldn't believe this was happening. I was both embarrassed and grateful.

When Rodney finished putting the spare tire on my car, the man told him to roll the tire across the street to the service station so they could repair it, and he told the man to clean up while he was there.

I thanked the man again. I was so astonished by what he did that I didn't even think to ask him his name. I told him I had better give my name to the people at the service station for my tire so I went across the street to the service station. I saw Rodney and thanked him again.

The service station attendant asked me who the man in the limo was. I didn't have the slightest idea. He said he watched the whole thing and couldn't believe it. Neither could I. I wish I had asked him his name, but I was flabbergasted at the time and I didn't.

Another time during a blizzard I slid off the road on a curve and wound up in the ditch. I knew I would be stranded out there for hours before a tow truck could get there to tow me out. I hadn't called for a tow truck yet when a Good Samaritan in a four-wheel-drive truck with a chain came to my aid and pulled me back onto the roadway. There are still a lot of good people in this world.

At one time police handled snow complaints. If people had not cleared the snow off the walks in so many hours after the snow stopped, they were subject to arrest. I worked in an older part of town where most of the

I shoveled the snow for the two elderly women.

lots were fifty-feet wide and the houses were close to the streets. I had two elderly ladies who lived in my district who were not physically able to shovel their walks and didn't have any money to have it done for them. There were no organizations at that time to do it for them.

I first learned of these ladies when I was sent to their houses on snow complaints. They both lived in the smaller houses with the fifty-foot frontage. I wondered why some of their neighbors didn't help them. I soon learned some of the younger ones didn't bother to shovel their own walks. I understand why people who had to use the sidewalk complained. I talked to the people who hadn't shoveled their walks and took down their names. I told them they were in violation of the law, and I would have to get a warrant for their arrest if the walks weren't shoveled in four hours when I came back. All of the walks were clean.

I shoveled the snow for the two elderly women. It took about fifteen minutes. I only did it twice before someone else started doing it. I noticed all of the neighborhood sidewalks were cleared. I guess all the people needed was a little nudge to get them to do it.

Omaha's neighborhoods have their own identity, especially some of the older areas. I was working security part-time at the Florence Pioneer Days celebration. Florence was a city in Nebraska before Omaha was but Omaha grew faster than Florence did. In 1917 Florence was annexed by the City of Omaha and ceased to be a separate city. It is still referred to as the Florence area of Omaha. Once a year they celebrate Florence Days.

I walked past this Daniel Boone–looking guy dressed in buckskin clothing and wearing a coonskin hat. He had a black powder rifle, and he fired it over my head after I walked past him. He and his friend thought it was funny when I jumped. They were laughing so hard that they were crying.

I turned around and got right in his face and told him if he fired that gun one more time he was going to go to jail for discharging a firearm in the city limits, and I was going to confiscate his gun and he could explain to the judge why he did such a childish thing as to fire a gun over the back of someone's head.

Two more officers were there now and one of them said, "You heard the officer; he's giving you a break. You better go on home now before I put the two of you in jail." The two of them hightailed it down the street and I never saw them the rest of the weekend.

When I was first promoted to sergeant in the traffic section, I was assigned to attend meetings with different neighborhood groups concerning traffic-related problems. One neighborhood association had a real problem. A used car lot had started in their neighborhood about two years before and since then it had grown and grown.

The cars kept creeping out of the lot into the street encroaching into the residential area until there were no places left for the homeowners to park their cars. Neighbors had called the police continually. The police would mark the tires (to indicate if the cars ever moved), but the people from the lot moved them a few feet and nothing could be done then.

The neighbors talked to the lot owner and he was aware of their problem but nothing was ever done. The homeowners were tired of trying to find a place to park blocks away from their homes. Neighbors were upset with other neighbors for taking their parking spaces. I told them I would be upset too if I were them.

I told them I would like to try something different to take care of their problem, but I would need all of their help in court if the car lot owner tried to fight.

"I'm not going to tell you my plan yet, but I will keep your board member informed," I told the group.

I researched the law on operating a business on city property without a permit. One only had to show they were in fact operating their business on city property (in other words, parking their car inventory on city streets).

On the following Sunday night two officers and I tire marked all of the cars parked on the street around the lot with a blue chalk line instead of the yellow chalk on the top of the tire with a matching line on the wheel well. After seventy-two hours had passed, I called the radar crew to meet me at the car lot, and we towed in fifteen cars for violation of the dead storage ordinance.

When I came to work the next day I called the impound lot to see if anyone had claimed any of the cars we towed in. They said all of them belonged to the car lot. They had to prove they owned them before they could be released.

It cost the lot owner over $1,000 to get them back.

When I held roll call, I asked two of my biggest officers to meet me at the car lot in one hour. When we went inside the office, the owner was there.

He said, “I suppose you’re here to tow in the rest of my cars.”

> I told the officers to handcuff him because he was under arrest.

So I said, “We’re here to see your permit to operate a business on city property.”

“But I’m not operating a business on city property,” he responded.

“The fifteen cars you retrieved from the tow lot today tell a different story,” I said. “I’m going to advise you of your rights and then I’m going to arrest you for not having a permit. You can call your attorney after you are booked and tell him you need $1,000 to get out of jail. You can also tell him five of your neighbors are going to testify you tried to sell them cars while they were parked on the street.”

I told the officers to handcuff him because he was under arrest for operating a business on city property without a permit.

“The neighbors are tired of you running over them. It has been going on far too long and they are not going to put up with it anymore. They will be in court to appear against you,” I said.

His attorney must have advised him to plead guilty because we were never subpoenaed to appear against him in court. He moved the business shortly after that. I don't think the man liked me, but the people who lived in the neighborhood sure did.

- Twenty-One -

HITTING 10-7

I had been thinking about retirement and 1988 seemed like a good time. I had spent thirty years in law enforcement. The people had changed so much from the time I first came on the job. I knew there were still a lot of good people out there, but I wasn't coming in contact with them. We didn't pay into Social Security on the police job so I had to work a few more quarters to qualify for it. I had planned on collecting on my wife's, but the law was changed so we were no longer allowed to do that.

After I took my police pension, I worked until I qualified for Social Security and Medicare. The government reduced my Social Security benefits because I have the police pension, but I still have Medicare. I know some retired police officers who don't.

I became a part-time Public Safety Officer for the Metropolitan Community College for a year and then I traveled Nebraska and Iowa doing drug draws on male federal employees. I was teamed up with a female nurse. She was the team leader and did the drug draws on the female employees plus she caught any flack if something went wrong.

We tested mostly Department of Transportation employees: air traffic controllers, FAA inspectors, mine inspectors, highway safety inspectors, railroad safety inspectors, aircraft maintenance people and others.

My police background really prepared me for this job. A lot of the older people were embarrassed and mad. I was able to talk to them and I even became friends with some of them. Sadly some of them tested positive, but they cleaned up their act and stayed clean for the seven years I worked with the program.

My partner and I were the top team in the nation for several years. We made fewer mistakes, had fewer complaints, and always arrived at our scheduled times. I had more quarters in now than I needed for my Social Security. I told my partner that I was going to resign at the end of the month. She hated to see me go but she understood. It was just a few days later when she said I didn't have to resign because our company lost their contract with the government and we were all going to be laid off in two weeks. I felt better when I learned this.

Several years after I retired, my wife and I were at a barbecue party. The hostess escorted a couple over to our table and introduced them to us. The woman asked if I was a police officer. I said I was but that I was retired now.

She said, "You're my guardian angel."

I told her, "I've been called a lot of things before but never a guardian angel."

> "You're my guardian angel."

She asked, "Do you remember the accident you were at where the girl was thrown out of the car and she was lying in the street in the snow, and two men were trying to pull the fender out on their car so they could drive it? My leg was broken and I couldn't move. They were going to leave me there in the cold lying in the street and suddenly you were there. You checked me and called the rescue squad. You told the driver of the other car to get his registration and have a seat in your car. You stayed with me until the rescue squad came. You said you knew my dad."

I said, "I remember you now. You were going to go into the Navy when you graduated from high school." I asked her if she did.

She said she had been a medic on a helicopter and did two tours in Vietnam with the Marines before she got out. She said, "I'm serious about you being my guardian angel."

I didn't know what to say. I don't know why I happened to drive down that street when I did. Maybe it was divine guidance, but it does happen and I was in the right place at the right time to help her. I felt good about it and I know now there are still good people out there.

Toward the end of my career, I was working at the warrant desk so the regular crew could go next door for lunch. They normally brought their lunches and ate in the office, but that day was someone's birthday and everyone was going next door to help celebrate it.

I was in the office by myself when this rather large man in a Marine Corps uniform walked up to the desk and asked to talk to me. I thought he must be someone with a warrant that I had been looking for.

I said, "I'm Officer Hauger. What can I do for you?" I was expecting him to say he had a traffic warrant.

He said, "You don't remember me, do you?"

"I'm sorry but I don't."

"Do you remember the two boys in the apartment building that you chased down the hall and you caught one of them, and the other one got away?"

"Yes," I said, "I remember that was over eight years ago."

"I'm the one you caught. You asked me who I was and wrote my name and address in your notebook and I gave you the other boy's name and told you where he lived. You told me I didn't have any business in the apartment building and you were going to break my fingers if you saw me in there again, and then you swatted me on my rear with your club and told me to get out of there and to never come back."

I thought to myself I hope he doesn't want me to try to swat his rear again. If he had it would have been one short battle and I would have been the loser.

Instead, he wanted to thank me. He said he told his mother what happened when he got home and she said I gave him a big break. She told him if he didn't find some new friends he would wind up in jail the next time. He said he knew she was right so he listened to her.

He was able to make new friends in high school and enlisted in the Marines when he graduated from high school. He was going to college under the GI Bill and he is in the Marine Corps Reserves. He told me that I played an important role in his life in turning him around and he would never forget it.

I said, "Your mother must be very proud of you." I told him I was glad he was able to get back on track, but he was the one who did it. I remembered reading where his ex-friend, the boy who had been in the apartment building with him that day, was back in prison.

These were the events that made it all worthwhile, and there were many others.

I have purposely avoided writing about most of the blood and gore I have seen. We all see enough each night on TV. Believe me when I say it is far more graphic in real life. I have seen officers puke at crime scenes. I have felt like I was going to. It is nothing to be ashamed of. We are human beings just like everyone else. When I joined the department we were taught what happens on the job stays on the job. We did what we were taught to do and kept everything to ourselves.

When I begin writing this book things that I thought were forgotten years ago started coming back to me. I had buried them somewhere deep in my mind and now they were coming back on their own and it bothered me as much today as it did years ago when it happened. I realize the authorities were wrong in teaching us not to talk to anyone about the unnatural things we did and saw.

When I was in training, we started teaching the recruits that it was okay to tell their wives what they were doing

Officers no longer have to hide things that bother them like we did.

on the job. When the city first contracted a psychologist, I had some doubts. After talking to people who have used their service, I believe they are an asset to both the city and the police officer. Today officers no longer have to hide things that bother them like we did. They now have a place where they can go if they need help. I know good police officers who resigned and moved into other fields because the stress of the job became too much for them to handle by themselves. A police psychologist should greatly reduce this outflow.

When I look back at all of the different tasks I performed as a police officer, I find it hard to believe. I have picked up blood at the blood bank and expedited it to the different hospitals and hand carried it into the operating room where they were waiting for it. I made calls to the mental wards to assist them with unruly patients.

I worked security for different celebrities such as the Beach Boys, Perry Como, Liberace, Bob Hope, Tennessee Ernie Ford, and Jerry Lewis when they entertained at the Aksarben arena. I escorted President Ronald Reagan and his First Lady at different times and President George H.W. Bush.

I was in the north interceptor sewer of the city when it was under construction. The machinery used to construct it was amazing.

Thanks to the job I was on the nineteenth floor of the Woodmen tower when it was under construction before there were any exterior walls. The wind up there was unbelievable. I have no desire to do something like that again.

I have been in the bootlegger tunnels on the north side of town, which I never knew existed. No doubt there are many places where I have not been, but I have been in many places where few people will ever be.

We had our gangs then but our police chief at the time said we didn't have a problem. The street cops thought differently. When you compare the gangs we had then to the ones today, perhaps the chief was right. We didn't have a gang problem then. I can't help but think if we had taken action then perhaps we would not be having the problems we are having today.

We had a drug problem then and they have one now. Even with aggressive enforcement the problem seems to have gotten worse. Our present system is not working. It's time to try something different.

I would be remiss if I failed to say anything about the death penalty. The State of Nebraska has the death penalty. Across the bridge from us in Iowa there is no death penalty. During the time I was a police officer numerous murderers took their intended victims across the river into Iowa to do their dastardly deeds. This shows me that the death penalty is a deterrent to murder.

However, for years now there have been different attempts to abolish the death penalty in Nebraska for a variety of reasons. So far they have all failed. It is true the death penalty does not deter murder like it once did. To be effective the sentence must be carried out promptly after the suspect has been found guilty of the crime.

This is no longer done because one appeal after another is granted and heard by the courts. It often takes over twenty years for a death sentence to be carried out. It has reached a point now with all of the appeals where a life sentence with no chance for parole costs less than a death sentence does.

It is time for a change. Do we repair our faulty death penalty system or do we throw it out and go with the life sentence with no chance of parole? We the taxpayers have made some attorneys very wealthy paying them when they appeal these death penalty cases. Most people don't realize when the higher court hears one of these appeals, tax money pays: the prosecuting attorneys, the judges, the defense attorneys, the clerks, the witnesses, and everyone involved. One would think it is time for our lawmakers to step in and make some long overdue adjustments to the system.

When I became a police officer, only the blood test was recognized by the courts as a means of measuring a person's blood alcohol content. The breathalyzer estimates a person's blood alcohol concentration by measuring the amount of alcohol in their breath.

When we had a person suspected of driving under the influence (DUI), we radioed in to have ID warm up the breathalyzer. If the driver failed the breathalyzer test, he or she was transported to county for a blood test. The results of both tests were sent to the court so they could be compared.

When the court finally accepted the validity of the breathalyzer test, they gave the driver the choice of taking either the blood test or the breathalyzer. Since 2002 it has been illegal in all fifty U.S. states to drive with a blood alcohol concentration that is 0.08 or higher. At one time arresting officers were filming the drivers as they were given a sobriety test, but for some reason that practice was discontinued after a short period of time.

One thing I was told officers do today, that we never did, is write multiple charges for one violation. A good example is a DUI who hits a parked car and then runs over the curb before coming to a stop. The charge in my day was DUI. Why they are also charged today with following too close, for hitting a parked car, and a third time for driving over the curb. I do not understand their reasoning for doing this. It seems like the DUI charge would cover it all.

I have experienced things that only a few people will experience.

I have noticed the number of female officers who receive life-threatening gunshot wounds and somehow manage to survive them while the male officers continue to die from non-life-threatening gunshot wounds. Could it be their mindset caused by the games they played as children when one always dies when they are shot?

Being a police officer has made my life an interesting one. If I could live my life over, there would be little that I would change. I have experienced things that only a few people will experience. I have been places and seen things that I would never have been able to do if I had not been a police officer. I have rubbed shoulders with people from all walks of life and discovered there is good in the worst of people and there is bad in the best of people. And I've seen it all.

A Police Officer

I was that which others did not want to be.

I went where others feared to go
and did what others failed to do.

I asked nothing from those who gave nothing back,

and I reluctantly accepted the thought of
eternal loneliness should I fail in my endeavor.

I have seen the craggy face of terror,
felt the stinging cold of brute fear,

and occasionally enjoyed the sweet
taste of a moment's victory.

I have cried, pained, hoped,

but most of all, have lived times others
would say were best forgotten.

At least I can hold my head up high
and be proud of what I was,

a Police Officer.

- *Anonymous*

ABOUT THE AUTHOR

Vern Hauger retired from the Omaha Police Department as a police lieutenant with badge #3 after thirty years of service from 1958 to 1988.

During his career with the department he worked in all of the bureaus. He designed and implemented the original Field Training Officer program for the Omaha Police Department. He served as the Training Commander, Crime Lab Commander, traffic lieutenant, and lieutenant in charge of the police impound lot.

He holds a bachelor of science degree in criminal justice from the University of Nebraska at Omaha. He attended the Traffic Institute at Northwestern University in Evanston, Ill., to become a police training instructor, and he received his certificate to teach from the Nebraska Law Enforcement Training Center at Grand Island.

He also attended other specialized police classes at the University of North Florida in Jacksonville, Colorado State University in Fort Collins, The FBI Academy in

Quantico, Va., and the Nebraska Law Enforcement Training Center in Grand Island.

He served on the Educational Committee of the Nebraska Crime Commission. He also served on the board of the Omaha Metropolitan Police Welfare and Benefit Association, Trustee on the Fraternal Order of Police board, the Executive Board of the Police Officers' Association, and the police and fire pension board. It was his way of paying back for all that he had received through the years.

Vern was born in 1934 during the Great Depression in Bartlett, Iowa, and spent the first two years of his life on a farm in Mills County, Iowa, before his parents gave up farming and moved to the big city of Omaha, Neb.

Vern was educated by the Omaha Public School System. He enlisted in the U.S. Air Force in June 1953 with a ninety-day delayed entry date. During that time period a cease-fire agreement was signed with North Korea, but most importantly he met the love of his life, Myrta (known as Myrt), at his friend's home when he went over to see him on the Fourth of July in 1953.

His parents were friends of her parents, and she had come with them for dinner. Vern had seen her in high school, but they never met and she hadn't noticed him. She noticed him that day and they dated every day until he left for the service. He came home on leave six months later and they were married. She went with him back to Texas where he was stationed.

Their next wedding anniversary will be the fifty-ninth. They raised four sons and have three grandchildren and two great grandchildren. Vern and Myrt are on the Board of Directors of the Florence Historical Foundation and are members of the Florentine Players.

Florence was a city in Nebraska before Omaha became one, but Omaha grew faster and annexed Florence in 1917. The Historical Foundation owns and maintains five historical properties: the Historical Florence Bank (1856, first bank in Nebraska), the Florence Train Station (1878 to 1966), the Historical Fire Station (1880, Fire Hose Company), the Mormon Bridge toll house (1953), and the land where the Florence City Hall and jail once stood.

A new Reception Hall was built on this property, and it is named the Florence City Hall. It is rented out to raise funds to maintain the other historical properties. As a public service some local groups meet there for little or no cost.

The Florentine Players is a part of the Historical Foundation. They put on shows in the hall because they enjoy doing it and hopefully to raise money for the foundation. Vern was one of the players, but today he is happier working in the kitchen than on the stage. Vern also writes articles for the Florence historical paper and dons his Santa Claus suit at the open house in the Historic Florence Bank each December so the kids can talk to Santa. Each receives a gift and their parents can take pictures. Santa also enjoys it.

Santa welcomes the children at the Historic Florence Bank.

www.ingramcontent.com/pod-product-compliance
Lightning Source LLC
Chambersburg PA
CBHW031827090426
42741CB00005B/160

* 9 7 8 1 9 3 6 8 4 0 2 8 1 *